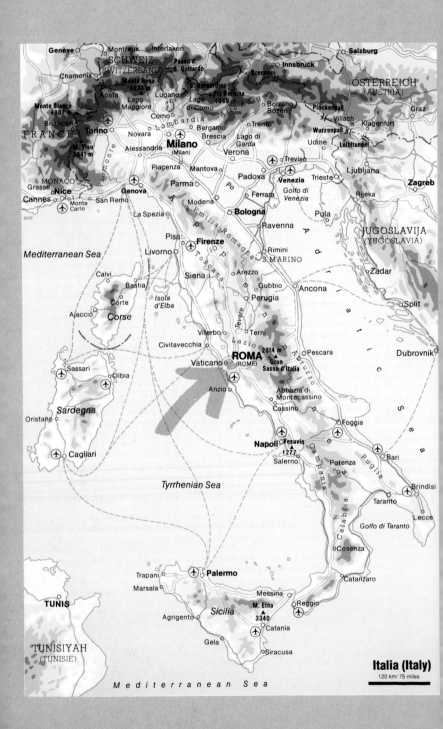

Italia (Italy)
120 km/ 75 miles

Benvenuti!

Imagine you have a friend in Rome, a companion who knows and loves this picturesque city, someone who will take you by the hand, guiding you through its history, culture, sights and exiting nightlife.

Veit Mölter, your *cicerone* in Rome, has lived on the banks of the Tiber for 22 years. His work as a correspondent with several daily newspapers has fired his interest in politics, led him to pay regular visits to the Vatican and to explore that cultural territory in which the Italians still reign supreme. Umberto Eco, Alberto Moravia, Giacomo Manzu or Federico Fellini—Veit Mölter knows them all. For the readers of this guide he has compiled walks and tours with his personal viewpoint very much in mind, to give visitors an insider's impression of the city.

Rome represents three thousand years of unbroken history, and it is this history, plus the legends surrounding the *caput mundi*, which is first on the agenda of *Insight Pocket Guide: Rome*. Three walks follow, to get you into trim in the first few days. All of them have specific themes: Day 1 is designed as an introduction, a view of the living Rome, a cross-section through the many-layered old city; the second day contains an encounter with the ancient world, and the third a visit to the Pope's hundred-acre kingdom.

An 'archaic smile' or a 'divine puzzle', a trip to the fountains of the Villa d'Este in Tivoli or a prowl through Rome's nightlife scene—all these can be found in the range of optional excursions to be chosen and combined as you wish. The final section contains all the practical information necessary for the visitor to Rome.

Insight Pocket Guide: Rome does not set out to be the One True Guide. The Eternal City is inexhaustible and illimitable, made up of countless layers and seething with never-ending vitality. For this reason Veit Mölter has aimed at a wide readership—from culture-vultures and highbrows, to hedonists; the city on the Tiber has something for everyone.

Benvenuti! Welcome!

3

Insight Pocket Guide

Rome
First English Edition

INSIGHT *pocket* GUIDES

ROME

Author	**Veit Mölter**
Co-author	**Margit Bornmann**
Art Director	**Willi Friedrich**
Photography	**Elvira d'Ippoliti and**
	Mark Aurel Reitenbacher

INSIGHT
pocket
GUIDES

Contents

Maps

Dear Reader!

It is perfectly possible to have more than one father, but there is only one 'Mamma'. 'Seek the ancient mother', was the advice of the Delphic oracle to Aeneas after he had been made homeless in the destruction of Troy. You can find out the results of the search in Virgil; the hero's tribe founded Roma, the feminine reflection of Amor, god of love, on the seven hills above the mouth of the Tiber. A goddess, then, a belly, the 'ancient mother'. Rome is greater than London, Paris or New York. Learning Latin or Romanic languages, going into a Catholic church, studying art or law; sometime, somewhere, you will always encounter the 'mother'. In the **pietà romana**, a custom practised along the Tiber until the last century, young mothers suckled not only their babies at their breasts, but toothless old men as well.

'Noble simplicity and serene greatness'—Winckelmann's classicist ideal of beauty always did get on my nerves. Ancient history has nothing to do with being ethereal and anaemic, neither is it just a figment of the imagination; it is real and alive.

When I was a little boy I spent my holidays at Aunt Marie's, in a small village on the former border between East and West Germany. The patron saint of Schönau on the Brend is St Laurence. Every year, on 10 August, the villagers commemorate him with processions and cakes. Every year the same punch–line rang out from the pulpit. Laurence, awaiting a martyr's death over glowing coals, said to his tormentors, 'Turn me over, this side of me is done.' I now live on the site of his 'barbecue' of AD258. And the rack preserved as a relic under the window of San Lorenzo in Lucina is supposed to be the very one used on that occasion, although it's actually too small to roast a grown man.

In 1665 the painter Nicolas Poussin was buried in San Lorenzo. Some years ago, the Academie Francaise in Rome wanted his

bones, and the logical place to look was under the sublime marble monument to his name. In the crypt, our torches revealed a scene quite different from that we had expected. Piles of bones washed into every corner of the crypt by centuries of floods; lead coffins, overturned and full of holes; a whole tract of chambers overflowing with human remains; the only way to get from one chamber to another was to clamber impiously over the bones. Poussin was impossible to identify. Marble above, human humus below; another side of Rome. The Eternal City isn't always romantic, the Vatican rarely encourages a mood of faith. As the saying goes, *Roma venuta, fede perduta*—come to Rome and lose your faith.

Everyone is born without being consulted on the matter, but the actual process of becoming a human being is a little more complicated. Elective and spiritual affinities play their part in it as well. My formative experience took place during my studies in Italy. It was a Saul to Paul-type conversion, full of that euphoria produced by pushing back the frontiers of one's knowledge, full of pleasure in the good food and the elegant clothes; in addition, the Romans' casual, unconstrained way of approaching tradition and history was—and is—a constant source of fascination to me.

Scratch any Italian artist, designer or creator of fashion, and you'll uncover the ancient world, the Renaissance, the classicist elements which are ever-present even today—not as non–committal feelings, but vital and real, part of the quality of life. That's why I stayed here on the Tiber when many of my colleagues upped sticks after a few years' service. The 'ancient mother' as an object of study; as Eichendorff put it, 'the old song plays on and on, you never reach the end.' Rome to me is like destiny; it can be pleasurable, must be borne and has to be accepted. But, as a neighbour of mine, the writer Italo Calvino, told me, there's no need to worry; the Eternal City can easily manage to cope with chaotic traffic conditions, building speculators and corrupt councillors; 'the main thing is that she rediscovers her gods.'

The following pages are intended to help you search for them. I dedicate this book to my good friend Manfred Schmidt.

HISTORY

Bite of the She-Wolf

Dawn, 21 April, 753BC Romulus hitches the white oxen up to the plough to begin the foundation of his city. Jupiter himself has recommended the Palatine and communicated his advice through the flight of birds. Romulus draws a ritual furrow around the hill in the shape of a square. *Roma quadrata*, this was the heart of the empire which was to stretch from Britain to Persia and whose language was to become known as far away as Latin America. Every year the city's birthday is celebrated by a ceremony on the Capitoline. Pressure is growing in the Italian parliament to make Latin the first foreign language taught in elementary schools.

Why is the city called Roma? Juno was the goddess of femininity, and the Palatine was the seat of worship of a particularly buxom version of Juno, known as Rumina. In addition, the she-wolf which

La lupa romana

Culture

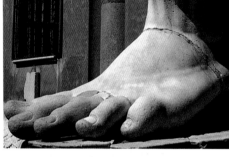

Emporer Constantine's foot

fished Romulus and Remus out of the Tiber, into which they had been pushed by a wicked uncle, suckled them at her *rumina*, or breast. Linguists agree that from there it's only a small step to Rome.

All roads lead to Rome, ran a later saying, although at this particular cradle stood a *lupa* baring her teeth, visible today in the Capitoline Museum as one of the oldest known hollow-cast bronze statues in existence. A perfect symbol for a city with a bite to it, as is the austere bronze likeness of Brutus, who liberated the state from the tyrannous Etruscan king Tarquinius in the year 509BC and who is the ultimate example of the 'Roman type'.

Wells which even today supply countless fountains in the city with cool drinking water; the Palatine, a hill fortress and easy to defend; the Tiber, a waterway leading to the sea and to salt-works, whose products were transported along the Salaria (Salt Road) for trading in Central Italy—all these advantages were included in the gift of the gods. And heaven got itself involved, as it does every time a foundation stone is laid. The uniting of divine loins and mortal flesh was not exactly rare in ancient times, and mythology is peopled with a whole host of demigods, including Romulus and Remus themselves. Their mother Rhea Silvia was a Vestal Virgin whose duty it was to guard the sacred flame; one day, the phallus of Mars emerged from the fire, and impregnated the virgin. Aeneas, the progenitor of the Roman people, was born as the consequence of a similar dalliance after Achilles' defeat of the Trojans; he was the fruit of the union of Anchises and Venus Genetrix. Later, Caesar was to erect a temple in his forum to this first mother of the Julian clan.

'Such a great city owes its origins to providence', opined Livy, Augustus' court historian. However, a sneaking suspicion remains that perhaps the facts came first and then the stories were invented to fit them. After all, the Romans were first and foremost practical types, and their first great deed was the construction of the *cloaca maxima* in the sixth century BC, whose 4-metre (13-foot) high barrel vault for disposing of the city's waste is still in use today.

Streets, Bridges, Water Conduits

The Romans were sceptical about speculative flights of fancy, but valued the down-to-earth. Take the legions, the most successful infantry in the whole of the ancient world. There may have been greater commanders, like Pyrrhus leading the Greeks, who won such a crippling victory over the Romans; or the Carthaginians under Hannibal, who left 50,000 Romans dead on the battlefield of Cannae in 216BC after crossing the Alps. In spite of their less-than-100 percent record, they still taught manners and morals to Etruscans, Greeks, Phoenicians, Gauls and Germans—a tribute to their indestructible team spirit.

'Woe to the defeated!' threatened the Gallic prince Brennus in 390BC when he succeeded in advancing as far as the Capitoline. And the legionaries of the time also acted according to prevailing martial law; Corinth and Carthage were plundered and destroyed, the conquered army leaders and kings (and the Gaulish hero Vercingetorix) were led through the forum in a triumphal procession and then executed, while less prominent prisoners were sold as slaves. Nevertheless, the Romans never showed the arrogance of a chosen people. They were pragmatists and adopted whatever spirit was in the air, giving hard workers a fair chance despite all social barriers. 'Once the slaves have gained their freedom', Philip V, King of Macedonia, noticed with surprise in 214BC,'they are accepted as citizens. Thus the citizens have increased the size of their city and founded 70 colonies.' When Caesar defeated Gaul with fire and the sword in 51BC, he forestalled new uprisings by appearing as a generous victor. The *pax romana* reigned for almost 400 years. In 418 the Romans, hard-pressed by Germany, withdrew their troops from Britain; the population set up a universal cry of protest, because the soldiers were so popular.

A multinational state with over 80 religions: not violence, but agreement born out of tolerance was the bond which held the empire together for so long. When Alarich and his Western Goths occupied Rome in 410, Saint Augustine wept for the end of a world. In 476 Odovakar,

The Esquiline Venus

The Dying Galatean

leader of the Germans, overthrew the last emperor, Romulus Augustulus. While the East Roman empire, with Constantinople as its capital, survived up to the Turkish onslaught of 1453, it was Rome that fired the imagination as a vision of the ideal.

On Christmas Day, AD800, Charles, King of the Franks, was crowned Emperor in St Peter's Cathedral. A new Roman Empire was born; this time it bore the epithet 'holy', and was later to gain the title 'of the German Nation'.

The Head of the World

The Caesars were the personification of power, and power needs a stage. In Rome it looked as if the empire would be pretty badly off for suitable settings. Hermodoros of Salamis had built the first classical marble temple in 146BC—dedicated to Jupiter Stator, the god of valour in war. The temples to Vesta and Fortuna Virilis (Piazza Bocca della Verità) and of the republican forum (Largo Argentina) bear testimony to the Greeks' cultural hegemony.

The lack of further relics surviving from the republican period can be attributed to the fact that architecturally speaking, Rome was pure province. A maze of narrow alleys, the buildings of tufa or brick, and above them on the Capitoline a respectable Jupiter Optimus Maximus enthroned in a 'temple' garnished with brightly coloured terracotta. Nero's act of arson in the year 64 was nothing more than a brutal attempt at urban remodelling.

However, it was Caesar who began the real process of demolition and whose self-aggrandisement was symbolised in the form of his forum. A rectangle enclosed by a portico, his own equestrian statue as the centre and the temple of his ancestress Venus Genetrix as eye-catching boundary. Caesar, already a living god, would receive the Senate within this temple while standing motionless as a monument, defying all the rules of republicanism.

Power transports, creates haloes. Caesar, who studied at Rhodes, imported his form of rule from the east, just as later Imperial fora

15

The Roman Forum with view of the Palatine

were inspired by Greek monumental edifices. Exhibitionism in marble, each commissioner trying to outdo his predecessors. Augustus' buildings are larger than Caesar's, and Trajan beats Augustus hands down. Since the basis for this architectural madness was the Hellenic model, the whole patchwork of temples, colonnades, basilica and squares still gives the impression of being homogeneous.

Were the Romans mere imitators? Johann Gottfried von Herder said, 'On the Tiber no philosophical systems were invented, but many were practised and introduced into the law, the constitution, into active life.' The same applied to architecture, art, and politics; to be successful, it was necessary to be sober and realistic.

On the Ides of March AD44 (the 15th), a total of 23 stab wounds tore the reins of power from Caesar's hands. His brother-in-law Junius Brutus had arranged the conspiracy, thinking to rescue the republic from the absolutist monarchy threatening to swamp it. His idealist beliefs convinced him that he had the support of the people. 'Et tu, Brute!' accused the dictator, who covered his head and died under the statue of Pompeius, the man whom he, in his turn, had driven to his death four years before. Panic seized the assassins. They broke away from each other, leaving the bloody bundle behind in the new Senatorial Curia (behind the Church of S Anrea della Valle).

Further pieces of the Colossus of Constantine

The republican constitution was no longer relevant to Roman reality. The empire was subject to its own forces, required long-term planning and fast decision-making, which a system with annual elections of a new Head of State could not supply. The façade of democracy still remained, but behind it there lurked a nest of potentates who caused a chain of civil wars; first Marius versus Sulla, then Pompeius against Caesar or Antonius against Octavian.

The citizens became tired of the confusion, and Octavian Augustus staked his new Imperial position on the desire for peace and quiet. His claim to historical fame was the erection of statues of all the prominent ancestors from Aeneas onward on the Palatine, upon the very spot where Romulus' hut had once stood. Chatting to people in the street, wearing a toga woven by his wife Livia, a Caesar 'like one of us', who was yet omnipresent, since his likeness figured on coins and his statues graced public buildings.

Power likes to justify itself by citing 'divine right', and even a military rough diamond like Napoleon placed the crown on his head in the presence of the Pope. Virgil wrote, 'Now and henceforth, Apollo reigns',—well, if not actually Apollo, then at least Augustus, the god's son; the sundial built by the emperor—the largest ever constructed—then became the ideological manifesto of the ruler, together with the *ara pacis* and the mausoleum. On the bas-reliefs of the *ara pacis* (the Altar of Peace, now located at Lungotevere in Augusta) the emperor is portrayed as Pontifex Maximus, the High Priest. On Augustus' birthday, 23 September, day and night are the same length, symbolising his harmony and equanimity. On this day, the sundial's point (now located in the Piazza Montecitorio) casts a shadow whose tip points straight at the centre of the altar. The conclusion was clear: the path to peace began with Augustus, and with him, conceived at the winter solstice, a new, a golden age was to begin. The emperor came from heaven, and cleverly publicised miracles put any doubts to rest.

Palazzo Venezia

Bread and Circuses

The satirist Juvenal, who lived around the year 100, pointed out that during the republican era, Roman citizens placed a high regard on public service and played a full part in political life. But that had been some time ago; 'Now they don't give a damn, and greed has driven everything out of their minds but bread and circuses.' The number of days on which games or ceremonies were held, 77 towards the end of the Republic, had increased to 177 during the reign of the emperors. Why? 'A people that yawns', said the French historian Jérome Carcopino, 'is ready for a revolution. The Caesars never let the plebs start to yawn, either out of hunger or boredom. The games were simply and solely an absolutist instrument of power.' It should be added that Rome could only boast a permanent amphitheatre from the year 80, upon the completion of the Colosseum, because Vespasian's and Titus' predecessors had been afraid of uprisings; writers always portray the plebs as a natural phenomenon, moody and unpredictable. Animal hunts and gladiator fights are older than the emperors; as early as 216BC, 44 sword fighters had to do battle in the forum as part of the funeral ceremony of Marcus Antonius Lepidus.

The *ludi* were by no means a mere series of massacres. Romans included horse-racing, light and heavy athletics competitions and, above all, theatre in their conception of games. Cicero, who was a moralist, gave them a status far above mere 'opium of the people'; 'Roman citizens have three areas where they may air their opinions and desires: peoples' assemblies, elections, and games and gladiator fights.' As early as 200BC the plebs had been marked off from the patricians and dismissed to the back benches. In order to discourage promiscuity, Augustus, a strict ruler, followed this by segregating men and women—the women were banished to the very back. Entrance was always free, and during the republican era the spectacle was often sponsored by politicians as pre-election propaganda.

Junius Brutus

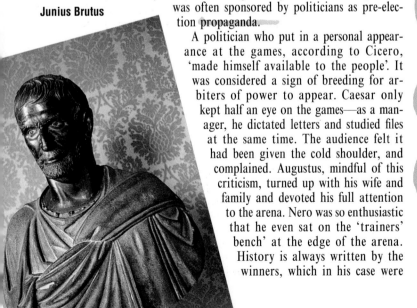

A politician who put in a personal appearance at the games, according to Cicero, 'made himself available to the people'. It was considered a sign of breeding for arbiters of power to appear. Caesar only kept half an eye on the games—as a manager, he dictated letters and studied files at the same time. The audience felt it had been given the cold shoulder, and complained. Augustus, mindful of this criticism, turned up with his wife and family and devoted his full attention to the arena. Nero was so enthusiastic that he even sat on the 'trainers' bench' at the edge of the arena. History is always written by the winners, which in his case were

The steps of the Palazzo Senatori

the persecuted Christians; but in the stadium, this emperor is still spoken of in tones of respect even now, a good two centuries later.

'Rome used to be a brothel, now it's a city', remarked Martial, notorious for his sharp tongue, about the Caesars' mania for building. Italy has around 12 million inhabitants, one million of whom reside in the capital. The invention of a process by which walls could be cast in situ in a material similar to concrete, producing masonry which was light but also indestructible, made bolder, more spectacular architectural designs possible. Take the magnificent bathing temples of the Thermae, for instance, of which there were 170 by Augustus' time, or the Circus Maximus, holding an audience of 225,000, which is still the greatest stadium ever built. Theatre fans could find satisfaction in the largest such establishment, that of Pompeius, with a capacity of 27,000 (La Scala in Milan holds 3,600). And 50,000 sadists could get their kicks simultaneously in the Colosseum.

The actor Esopos saved a few million sesterces, making him richer than many a senator. Victor, the driver of a team of horses, was rewarded for winning 429 races with large sums of money and the bestowal of civic honours. Circus day was also slaughter day. The inaugural celebrations of the Colosseum sent 5,000 animals to their deaths. Criminals were bound and thrown to the beasts, in some cases after being wounded slightly to spur the animals on. Rome's millennium celebrations in AD249 ended the lives of 32 elephants, 60 lions, 6 hippopotami, 10 tigers, the same number of hyenas, giraffes, elks and zebras, 20 donkeys, and 40 wild horses.

And that wasn't all; 2,000 gladiators marched into the arena with the cry 'Hail, Caesar, those who are about to die salute you!' Here there was no such thing as a draw: one in two gave up the ghost, either dead or severely wounded, thrown onto the mercy of the emperor or the audience and their thumbs-up or thumbs-down. Early chronicles contain accounts of a priest dressed as Charon, the

The Colosseum

ferryman of Hades; with one blow of a hammer on the forehead of the conquered gladiator, the priest either confirmed his death or assisted his passage into the realm of shadows.

Man cannot live on games alone; in the reign of Caesar, 150,000 citizens received free corn to make bread. In the year 367, 317,333 people were listed as being entitled to a free piece of pork. It was easy to see the unknown masses as threatening. Bloodthirsty in the arena, lazy at their work, and unpredictable into the bargain, prone to unrest if the supply ships were delayed by storms.

In those days there were no newspapers, opinion polls or political parties—the 'upper ten thousand' had no real idea who they had to deal with in the plebs. Nowadays historians show a little more consideration towards Ancient Rome's man in the street. The capital was certainly a concentration of extremes, but free hand outs of bread, olive oil, wine and meat were also the rule in Constantinople, Carthage, Antioch, Alexandria and many smaller communities. It was all part of the system.

Firstly, it wasn't the laziness of the people that forced the emperor to give them food. There were no industries, and the state bureaucracy only employed as many people as were absolutely necessary. The ruling class fed the populace because there was no work. This observation, however, does not take into account the considerable numbers of independent craftsmen and traders working on their own initiative. Romans regarded the state as the highest good. Anyone who was a free citizen belonged to the state, just as the human body is made up of head and limbs, each part dependent on the others. The payment of what was basically a sort of unemployment benefit was all part of the heathen *amor populi*.

Christian charity was driven by a different motivation from that of state assistance. It was chiefly engaged in good works in this 'earthly vale of tears', in order to mark up points for the hereafter. Those on society's fringes who fell through the net of official charity were caught by the *amor pauperum*—love for the poor.

The Return of the Gods

In 1506, 25 ancient sculptures were excavated from the Titus Thermae. Pope Julius II sent Michelangelo along to the site with the architect Giuliano Sangallo, who stood before the marble statue of Laocoon the priest entwined with snakes, and exclaimed in a state of rapture: 'This is the very work described by Pliny!' '...Laocoon, in the Palace of Titus, a work excelling all else in painting and sculpture,' wrote Pliny, the natural scientist who perished in the eruption of Vesuvius in AD79. And lo! That masterpiece by the Greek sculptors Hagesandros, Polyodoros and Athanodoros was in the public eye once more, exhibited in a place of honour in the Vatican.

Archaeology fever had struck. People began swinging down on ropes from the top of Trajan's Column to study the reliefs at close quarters. By chance, the subterranean chambers of Nero's 'Golden House' came to light, and Raphael and his consorts copied the wall decorations, which took all Europe by storm. Rome was a beacon of culture once again.

'Rebirth' (*renascimento*) was the name given by educated Italians to this rediscovery of ancient glories, and the abyss yawning between the two eras was dubbed 'the Middle Ages'. The blood of ancient times flowed so persistently in the veins of the Roman Middle Ages, however, that the city's Gothic cathedrals (of which only Santa Maria sopra Minerva has survived), never managed to convey that impression of yearning heavenward which is the key of the international Gothic movement. Instead they lay earthbound, confined to a horizontal plane. The essence of the Gothic movement, it must be concluded, remained beyond the Romans' grasp.

Iuvat vivere—living is delightful—was a key idea in the Renaissance. God descended from the highest heavens and revealed Himself in the creativity of man. The religion of beauty came along to accompany belief in Christ. The Popes awarded commissions to Raphael and Michelangelo, to those geniuses of the Baroque, Bernini and Borromini, to the Coryphaei of classicism, Canova and Thorwaldsen. The 'second Rome' had at last reached a stage of development where it could match the achievements of antiquity.

In the streets straightened out by Julius II and Leo X, it was clothes which once more made the man, and indeed the woman. Concordia della Valle strolled around in garments of silver brocade with golden belts and pearl-embroidered sleeves—'like Pallas Athene', mocked a chronicler of the time. All eyes were drawn to Sonisba Cavaliere in her cream velvet dress, yellow silk scarves and belts of antique coins. Ask today's fashion designers—Armani, for example or Versace—where they get their wonderful feeling for colour and harmony, and they'll tell you *unisono*, 'From the Renaissance, of course'.

Christian morals took a back seat. At a reception on 13 March, 1519, the list of those present included 'four cardinals, close relatives of the pope, three high-class whores and a load of fools'. The christening of an illegitimate son of the banker Agostino

Souvenirs for visitors from all over the world

Chigi featured 'such dishes as parrots' tongues, and fish brought alive from Byzantium. After each course, the guests took childish pleasure in flinging the golden plates and implements into the Tiber'—across which, however, a net had been stretched to catch them. Morals were loose, corruption rampaged, the popes favoured their own families. Martin Luther, living in the monastery on the Piazza del Popolo in 1510, fulminated against the 'Whore of Babylon'; 'I would never have believed that the papacy could be such a menace unless I had seen the Roman court with my own eyes.' And though Emperor Tiberius was worthless, he was 'an angel compared with the Roman emperor of today—when he dines, he has 10 naked girls standing before his table.' The naked girls are pure bunkum, and, what's more, the monk from Wittenberg 'had no access to the high levels of the Curia, he did not dine with cardinals' (Gregorovius) but usually spent his time with fellow Germans. He came along 'like a pilgrim from the Middle Ages journeying to Rome', which was just asking for misunderstandings and incomprehension; Luther was even less able to understand the sensuousness of the Renaissance than the Italians were able to understand the principles of Northern Gothic.

The Counter-Reformation saw Rome keeping its morals on a rather tighter rein; baroque art, however, exceeded all moral boundaries, was propaganda, seduction and open triumph in one. Let's stand on the stage of eternity for a second and marvel; it is this spirit, together with classicism, that has shaped the city of Rome, and even the more peculiar edifices such as the national monument to Victor Emmanuel, christened 'the luxurious *pissoir*' by the writer Papini, owe something of their style to their ancient predecessors. If you ask me, Goethe is still hanging around as well. Over on the Corso is his flat, now a museum; on the other side, in the Via, is the Osteria dell' Orso, where he first ended up and which nowadays is a haunt of the *jeunesse doree*. His lover's name was Faustina. During the day, he walked through Rome: "Throughout the nights Cupid keeps me busy in another way; I become only half a scholar, but twice as happy. And is this not learning, to study the forms of her lovely bosom, and slide my hands down over her hips? For I understand marble then all the better..."

22

HISTORY

BC

753 According to legend, Romulus founds Rome and becomes its first king.

509 Fall of the seventh king, Tarquiniius Superbus. End of Etruscan rule. Republic proclaimed.

387 Gauls conquer Rome.

241 Victory in the First Punic War: Sicily becomes a Roman province.

218 Second Punic War; Hannibal crosses the Alps.

216 Defeat at Cannae; Hannibal *ante portas* (before the gates).

202 Decisive victory over Hannibal in Battle of Zama ends war.

168 Victory at Pydna, defeat of the Kingdom of Macedonia.

146 Destruction of Carthage and Corinth.

133 Civil war starts with the murder of Tiberius Gracchus.

101 First clash with the Germans; Cimberi and Teutons wiped out.

71 Gladiatorial War led by Spartacus ends in bloodbath.

60 First triumvirate: Caesar, Pompeius, Crassus.

51 Caesar completes his conquest of Gaul.

44 Caesar assassinated.

43 Second triumvirate: Antonius, Octavian, Aemilius Lepidus.

31 Caesar Octavian Augustus assumes autocracy.

9 Danube border established.

AD

64 First persecution of Christians under Emperor Nero.

98 Trajan takes up office. The Empire is extended.

270 Aurelian builds a defensive wall round Rome.

286 Diocletian divides Empire's administration into east and west.

330 Constantinople becomes capital of the Empire.

410 Alarich, leader of the West Goths, plunders Rome.

452 Pope Leo the Great prevents Attila from conquering Rome.

476 End of the Western Empire.

546 Totila, king of the East Goths, conquers Rome.

800 Coronation of Charlemagne as Roman Emperor.

1144 Arnaldo of Brescia tries— like Cola di Rienzo later—to separate Rome from the papacy.

1300 Boniface VIII organises the first 'Holy Year'. Papacy at the height of its power.

1309 Clemens V chooses Avignon as his residence. Papacy falls under the influence of French kings.

1378 The 'Avignon exile' ends with the election of Urban VI of Rome. Clemens VII sets up as counter-pope.

1417 The election of Martin V ends 40 years of schism; the Pope is once again ruler of Rome.

1527 'Sacco di Roma'; German and Spanish merceneries plunder the city for months, 30,000 die.

1572 Gregor XIII begins restoration of ancient water pipes; the Roman fountain tradition begins.

1797 General Duphot raises the 'Roman Republic'.

1815 Restoration of the Roman Church State by the Congress of Vienna.

1860 A large part of the Church State falls to the kingdom of Italy.

1870 Rome, population 20,000, is conquered by Spanish troops and becomes capital of Italy.

1922 Fascists march on Rome. Mussolini becomes dictator.

1944 Allied troops march in on 4 July.

1957 The Treaty of Rome is signed on 25 March, laying the foundation for a United Europe.

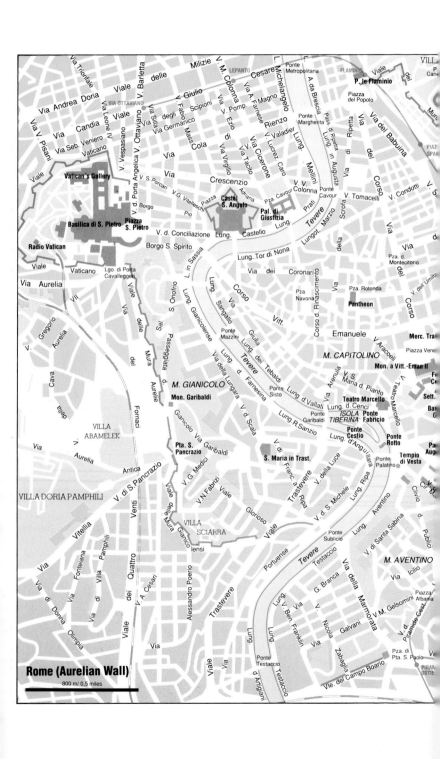

Rome (Aurelian Wall)

800 m/ 0,5 miles

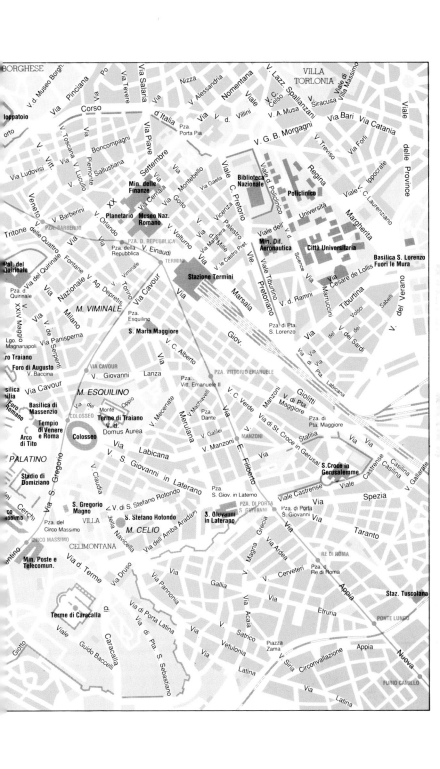

Day Itinerary

DAY ①

The Layer Cake of History

A little flirtation with Mamma Roma—the old city is 'the loveliest belly in the world'. Nibble on the 'mille feuilles' of history, look for affinities; there's bound to be something to appeal to you. Buon Giorno with Raphael and Bernini, Michelangelo and Borromini. There's no avoiding the sacred cows of art between Piazza Navona and Piazza del Popolo. Relax in the evening with the nightlife behind Navona.

Buses: Corso del Rinascimento (Senato) 26, 87, 186; Corso Vittorio Emmanuel (Palazzo Braschi) 46, 62, 64.

Which of the three cafés on **Piazza Navona** you start the day in depends on the season and the weather. The square is still empty at breakfast-time, but in the afternoons and on summer evenings it overflows with every possible manifestation of life—children, artists, fire-eaters and similar native fauna.

The Fountain of Four Rivers

Close your eyes for a second and travel back in time to the year 90. Caesar Domitian is there in his white toga with Domitia, his better half (who has him murdered six years later). The crowd is going mad at the start of the Formula 1 of the ancient world, Ben Hur's team of greys in pole position. Now open your eyes again. The shape of the square is the only surviving feature of the race,

Piazza Navona

but a *cappuccino* and *cornetto* (assuming you go for an Italian breakfast) make up for it. The aroma of genuine horse-droppings wafts from the top end of the square where the coaches stand.

Eyes to the centre; what's the best way to introduce Gian Lorenzo Bernini? A master of showmanship, tricks and jokes, a miracle man. Moses once smote water out of rock with his staff. Bernini manages much more than that with only a hammer and chisel. A palm-tree bends in the imaginary desert wind, water-snakes with death-dealing jaws rise out of the water where a lion is slaking its thirst. The fountain overflows with life—just look at the Danube and the Ganges, or the Nile, covering its head because its sources are still undiscovered, and the Rio della Plata, whose hand points, apparently in horror, to the Church of S Agnese in

27

Agone. Was Bernini trying to show his disgust at Francesco Borromini's pulsating church façade? Well, it's a nice story, but when the fountain was dedicated in 1651 the church unfortunately didn't exist—S **Agnese** was not completed until 1658. Bernini took the Pope for a ride in the unveiling ceremony by letting only the covers fall from the fountain—not one drop of water joined them. Innocent X had already turned on his heel in high dudgeon when he heard the sound of splashing behind him. Baroque beings just loved theatrical effects; the reaction? 'You have put ten years on my life'. Nevertheless, the Pope died earlier, in 1655.

Pietro da Cortona designed the façade of **S Maria della Pace**, in the Via of the same name, as a kind of stage set caught between being and seeming. But before our initial visit to Raphael, a different picture: the German national church of **S Maria dell' Anima** (after the Via S Agnese and Via Millina, turn right into Via della Pace, ring at the rear entrance) which still has the imperial-royal double-headed eagle perched on the top of its brightly tiled tower. Enter the church through a small courtyard with a little fountain. This is a hall church, basically Gothic in design and as high as it is wide. The church was delivered to Rome in the early 16th century as a German visiting card; however, the 'Anima', despite traces of German design still remaining, was transformed into an unmistakably Roman church—its cultural environment simply engulfed it.

Hadrian VI, who is buried in the Anima, was the last foreign Pope before Karol Wojtyla and represented precisely this sort of north–south rift. On his election in 1522, he walled up the medallions painted by Raphael, and the sight of the Laocoon statue inspired him to nothing more than the exclamation; 'Heathen images of idols!' The **altar of the Holy Family** was painted by Giuliano Romano, a pupil of Raphael. Next, go past the front of the 'Pace' Church to the entrance of Number 5, the **Arco della Pace** (open Monday–Wednesday, Friday 10am–1pm and 3–5pm; Saturday

28

10am–1pm), through the **monastery courtyard** built by the Renaissance maestro Bramante (entrance through the sacristy). On the left above the last chapel you'll see **Raphael's Four Sibyls**. Heathen fortune-tellers—what can they be doing in a church? One of them, the 'Tiburtine', is said to have prophesied that a child would come and rule the world. There is a similar passage in Virgil (Emperor Augustus took it to refer to himself), and for Renaissance ideologists statements like these were grist to their mill.

The Sibyls as Old Testament prophetesses, the ancient world as a divinely ordained prologue to the birth of Christ; that was enough to forge the link. Michelangelo painted the girls in the Sistine Chapel, Dante chose Virgil as his guide in the *Divine Comedy* as early as 1311. Before heading back to Navona, have a drink in the **Antico Caffe della Pace** (open at 11am), in great demand as a film set. If you look around the area you will find antiques in the **Via Coronari** (90m/100yds from Arco della Pace), metal-work in the **Via Panico** and streets around it, and carpenters in Vicolo delle Vacche—**La Sedia** (No 9a) has every kind of chair imaginable. **Vetro Creare** (Piazza S Salvatore in Lauro 3) will make coloured windows and glass doors to your design.

On the other side of Navona is the **Palazzo Madama**, named after Margarethe of Austria, the illegitimate daughter of Charles V. A powerful woman, who was more or less forced into marrying the much younger Ottavio Farnese, but who refused to countenance entertaining her husband's desires. The Pope, the emperor, even Loyola all tried to change her mind about consummating the marriage. Finally, after six years, she relented, and gave birth to twins in 1545; one of them, Alessandro, became a great general.

The Pantheon

Pass the palazzo, seat of the Senate, on your left, and go along the **Corso del Rinascimento** until you come to a sign reading **Archivio di Stato**. No need to worry about the policemen at the entrance; just go past and into the courtyard with its two-floor loggia (Giacomo Della Porta, 1587). Here is another of Borromini's strokes of genius: the pointed spiral tower of the church of S Ivo— unfortunately, as a rule, the church is closed. Leave the courtyard by the dark alley on the

Baroque craftsmanship

right at the back, continue down the Via Digana Vecchia till you come to S Luigi dei Francesi.

In this church you will find three real mega-hits of pictures in the fifth side chapel on the left: St Matthew with the angel, his calling (left) and his martyrdom (right). Try to imagine this painter being a gambler, a hooligan, a murderer, even? For Caravaggio (1573–1610) lived under constant threat of the gallows. Be that as it may, this realist, who hated academic idylls and who constructed his pictorial dramas using sophisticated plays of light and shade, was a giant among painters, and this gained him the support of the powerful Colonna family as long as he lived.

We continue into the Via Ciurtiniani or Piazza Sant' Eustachio to arrive at the **Pantheon**, the best-preserved of all the Roman temples, despite being continually gutted by a series of popes. Urban VIII, for instance, had the 23½-tonne bronze girders of the entrance hall melted down to make 100 cannons for the Monte d'Angeli and the pillars for the Bernini canopy in St Peter's. But still, the harmonious design of this temple, built in the reign of Emperor Hadrian, remained unclouded. The dome, built of progressively lighter material towards its apex, symbolises the canopy of the sky, its central opening the life-giving sun. The nave is 39m (129ft) high and wide and was designed along the principle of a hemisphere. It is thought that the Pantheon was not dedicated to 'all' gods, but to the 'All-Divine' itself. If you haven't had enough yet, take a short diversion to the left, past the Pantheon, to the **Elefantino Berninis** and **S Maria sopra Minerva**; **Michelangelo's Christ** is to the left of the altar; to the right, in the **Carafa Chapel**, are the famous **frescos of Filippino Lippi** (1498)—pure, unadulterated Renaissance.

Now is the right time to start thinking about lunch. One of the best fish restaurants in Rome is **La Rosetta**. Turn your back on the Pantheon, and go to the left into Via della Rosetta No 9 (about 90,000 lire). You can get typical Roman cuisine with carafe wines from the *castelli romani* in **Antonio**, Via dei Pastini 12 (on the right from the Pantheon, 20,000 lire). If you're looking for something cheaper, you can drink excellent wine and nibble delicious snacks in **Spiriti** in Via S Eustachio 5 (left) or cross the Via della Rosetta to the Via degli Uffici del Vicario. **Giolotti** is not only one of the best ice-cream parlours in Rome, but provides a fine self-service midday menu as well. For post-prandial relaxation go from Giolotti to the **Piazza di Montecitorio**. The obelisk used to be the pointer of Augustus' sundial. Behind it, in the **Piazza Colonna**, is the **Pillar of Marcus Aurelius**, a band of reliefs. Pass the Art Nouveau **Galleria Colonna** to the **Trevi Fountain**, and throw a coin backwards over your left shoulder into the fountain, so that the gods will allow you to return to Rome.

Go down the Via della Stamperia towards the Piazza di Spagna, climb the steps to the Trinità dei Monte, continue down the street of the same name to the left, and stop in front of the **Villa Medici**; Goethe sketched the fountain here in 1787 in exactly the same setting. After about 183m (200yds) you'll find a footpath on the right-hand side of the road sloping gently uphill to Pincio. Visit the neoclassical **Casino Valadier**, then enjoy the sunset and the view across the city to St Peter's from the Piazzale Napoleone I.

The day ends in the alleyways behind Navona. In the area around the Caffè della Pace you'll meet mostly Romans—no flash fashion, just reasonable prices. On the Piazza del Fico is **Da Francesco**, a pizzeria and ristorante with Roman cuisine, and **Corallo** (Via del Corallo 10). **Navona Notte** (Via del Teatro della Pace 44) serves only spaghetti and pizza. **Pancotto** (Via Tor Millina 17) provides elegiac piano music as an accompaniment to the food. **Jonathan's Angels** (Via della Fossa), a *Caffeteria*, wallows in Victorian keepsake-album kitsch and boasts of having the most grandiose antique toilets in the Eternal City.

Siesta time

Encounter with the Ancient World

The hub of the universe; an audience with the Emperor Marcus Aurelius on the Capitoline. The marble quarry of the Forum and Palatine. Gooseflesh in the Colosseum.

Buses: Piazza Venezia 9, 44, 46, 56, 57, 60, 62, 64, 65, 70, 85, 87, 90, 91, 94, 95, 204, 710, 718, 719. Taxi to 'Ara Coeli'

'God and master' was how Emperor Domitian saw himself. Anyone faced with Rome's unique brand of traffic chaos will soon form a different opinion, but if you want breakfast, you'll find the Imperial ruins spread out at your feet from the roof garden of the **Hotel Forum** (Via Tor di Conti 28). Mere mortals will find **Alexander's Snack Bar** (Piazza Ara Coeli) to their liking and will have the advantage that the *Direttissima* to the Capitoline is nearby. Even higher, at the top of the Capitoline, the staircase to the left leads to the 'Altar of Heaven' (**Ara Coeli**), a church dedicated to Our Lady with a chapel (**Cappella di S Bernadino**), on the immediate right painted by Pinturicchio in 1485.

He was a master of subtle brushwork whose subject matter was as visionary and unworldly as the ivory tower of the intellectuals. Alexander VI, who sent his beautiful daughter Lucrezia into one marriage bed after another as a pawn in his own domestic brand of power politics, chose Pinturicchio, of all people, as his court painter. The 'lecher Pope' and the shrinking violet—a quirk of history. How Luther fulminated about the Borgian Pontifex! But when you stand before the pictures now, all this has vanished. Art has proved to have more staying-power than such base passions.

If you take the side exit on the right and go down the steps you come to the **Piazza Campidoglio**. Don't be alarmed if you're greeted with loud applause by a wedding party. You haven't gatecrashed the wrong party—you're simply in the registry office

Piazza del Campidoglio

Palazzo Senatori

next to the museum, with a wedding turnover reminiscent of a conveyor-belt. In the courtyard are the colossal remains of a statue of Constantine. Michelangelo designed the Piazza, and used a couple of tricks to give an impression of space and size to a relatively small area; he avoided parallel lines and right-angles, extended the façades into a trapezoid shape and emphasised the view of the **Senatorial Palace** with a flight of steps and the Fountain of Minerva. The star pattern in the cobblestones originally had Marcus Aurelius at the centre of the piazza; now only the plinth is left, and the emperor himself has galloped away from the ravages of air pollution into the safety of the museum.

The main attraction here is the panoramic view of the **forum**. The Mayor of Rome can enjoy the view from his desk, even in the dark; one press of a button and the ancient remains are illuminated down to the last chipping. Go up the steps on the right to the glass frontage with door, through the building and out to the tiny park of the Via Tempio di Giove. You are standing on the **Tarpeian Rock**, from which consuls would push traitors with their own hands. On the left are the remains of the **Eight Columns of the Temple of Saturn**, once the safe of the State Treasury; Caesar got his hands on 15,000 gold ingots, 30,000 silver ingots and 30 million sesterces!

A further historical film-clip is on the programme here if you look down to the forum and imagine you are witnessing a triumphal procession. This incredible spectacle was mounted in honour of any general who had declared war, pushed forward the boundaries of the Empire and succeeded in killing over 5,000 of the enemy. The procession approached from the **Circus Maximus** and entered the Forum through the **Arch of Titus**; those taking part included senators, sacrificial animals, musicians, soldiers and of course the 'Imperator', all done up like Jupiter with his face painted with red

On the Palatine

lead, wearing a purple toga and laurel wreath. The spoils and the important prisoners led the way, followed by the quadriga, bedecked with laurel and drawn by white horses.

The conquered leader was presented as a mirror-image of the conqueror; Jugurtha also marched over the basalt slabs of the Via Sacra in kingly robes, but with bound wrists. Vercingetorix, Prince of Gaul, was incarcerated for six years until Caesar had time to celebrate his capture. The parting of the ways took place at the Temple of Saturn. Only a few metres further on the executioners strangled the losers in the Mamertine Cellar. The victorious general would then climb to the Capitoline to carry out the sacrifices. A state slave gave him the ritual warning, 'Look behind you! Never forget your mortality!'

We now go down the Via Tempio di Giove, then turn left to the **Tabularium** (78BC), the archive of both ancient and present-day Rome. Then we go up again to the **Musei Capitolini** (9am–1.30pm, Sunday 9am–1pm; Tuesday and Saturday also 5–8pm; closed Monday). The oldest museum in Europe, founded by Sixtus IV in 1471, is a 'we stock everything' establishment with imposing state chambers and a picture gallery with works by Bellini, Caravaggio, Rubens, Van Dyck, Velazquez and Veronese, among others. There are reasonable copies of Greek masterpieces as replacements for the lost originals: the *Capitoline Venus*, the *Dying Galatean* (sometimes incorrectly called the Dying Gaul), the *Wounded Amazon*.

Marcus Aurelius, gleaming with gold bronze, stands ready to receive you in the **Palazzo Nuovo** opposite. He is wearing the travelling dress of a senator, and has the ignorance of the Christians to thank for the fact that he is still on his travels; they mistook him for Constantine and didn't bother to melt him down. Once he had come down off his high horse for restoration, his features could be examined at close quarters. A proud man, the corners of his mouth turned down sceptically, deliberation in his eyes. All the

The temple of Venus and Rome

melancholy and loneliness of the powerful is expressed in him; 'A little time—and you forget everything. A little time—and everything forgets you', wrote the Emperor.

Looking around the Capitoline Square may bring the faint strains of Liza Minelli singing the refrain 'Money, money, money,' to your ears. Once, the Temple of Juno Moneta (the Warner) stood on the site of the **Aracoeli Church**. When coinage was introduced, the product received the goddess' name, which in turn became our word 'money'.

The way to the Forum goes off to the left past Senators' Square. But watch out for the tricks of the ancient world; 'I asked for bread, and ye gave me a stone!' So retrace your steps to the breakfast bar, and from there take the first alley to the left; **Anelino a Tor Margana** (Piazza Margana 37, 40,000 Lire) cultivates Roman cuisine within the walls which once saw Goethe partaking of refreshment (tables outside, closed Sunday). You'll get excellent fish in **Marios** (Piazza del Grillo 9, closed Sunday, 55,000 lire) and **Gamela** (Via Frangipane 34, closed Monday, 35,000 lire) on the other side of the Via dei Fori, with which Mussolini

The Arch of Constantine

covered over part of the imperial fora.

Along this thoroughfare you'll also find the entrance to the **Republican Forum** (9am–sunset, Sunday 9am–1pm). By the steps and along the road is the **Mamertine Prison**, where Peter and Paul did time, the baroque church of **S Luca e S Martina** and the back view of the **Arch of Septimus Severus** dating from 203, with marble reliefs bearing a strong resemblance to a lump of Parmesan; exhaust gases have wiped the faces off the defeated Parthians and Arabs. If you are a culture vulture, you can rent an 'acoustic guide' (Walkman) at the entrance of the forum for 8,000 lire, which will supply you with information on the Curia of the 300 senators, Romulus' grave with its black marble cover, the Basilica Julia, Castor and Pollux, the Vestal Virgins, the Temple of Romulus, the Basilica of Maxentius, and also on buildings which have been closed to the public for years. The information plaques on the monuments themselves are miserably insufficient.

You can also just walk around and look, thus avoiding the danger of not being able to see the Forum for the columns. At the Arch of Titus, commemorating the destruction of Jerusalem in the year 70, go up to the right to the **Palatine** and the **Farnesian Gardens** with their grotto of nymphs, fountain, pavilions and villa. The Renaissance put new heart into the old designers' maxim that less is more; the villa is more attractive and delicate than the Imperial works which inspired it. The Empire loved monoliths. The palaces of Augustus, Septimius Severus, and the Flavians are on a gigantic scale, making Romulus' walls look like a dolls' house. From the Founders' House (on the slope behind the gardens) a subterranean passage leads to the rear of the **Colosseum** (9am–4pm; Sunday, Wednesday 9am–1pm).

We can follow in the footsteps of the gladiators: the heroic draftees marched into the amphitheatre through the gate at the forum end, the losers were carried out through the opposite gate, the **Porta Libitinaria** (Libitina was the goddess of death). The maze of corridors and chambers under the arena had a solid wooden ceiling filled with sand. The Tribune of Caesar was at the centre of the eastern flank (in other words, on the left).

The Marquis de Sade was thrown into raptures on his visit to

Forum, with House of the Vestal Virgins

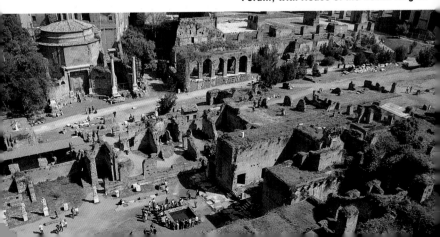

The Colosseum

Rome in 1775 as he stood in the Colosseum and marvelled the statistics: 10 years of bone-breaking work for 15,000 men, including many Jewish slaves; 76,455m³ (100,000 cubic yards) of Travertine stone, 272 tonnes of iron clamps. At its longest point 172m (564ft), at its widest 142m (466ft); an area of 2,807m² (30,214 square feet), 45m (150ft) high, 80 exits for 87,000 spectators. The view from the terrace at the top was as scary as the same position nowadays in a football stadium. Once, at the opening in the year AD80, two ships engaged in a naval battle in the arena. The amphitheatre was covered by a silk canopy, hoisted before every spectacle by a company of sailors. The ground floor of the Colosseum—named after a 105-ft (32-m) high bronze statue of Nero, which Vespasian set up in front of the arena and transformed into a sun god by the simple expedient of changing the head—can be visited for free; entrance must be paid for the upper level.

Every Good Friday the pope starts out from here to trace the stations of the cross. It is possible that Christians were thrown to the lions, but there are no actual records to confirm this. No-one believed it until the late 17th century, when Benedict XIV was the first to consecrate the arena to the blood of the martyrs. The **Arch of Constantine**, a collage concocted of artistic set-pieces depicting scenes from the more glorious past, is the counterpiece of the 'skull of antiquity' (Fellini on the Colosseum).

If you want to end the day in the same heavenly style in which you began it—and at the same price level—the roof terrace of the **Hotel Hassler** above the Spanish Steps has a fine restaurant. But not everyone 'was born in a shirt' (a Roman expression indicating a fat wallet), so here are a couple of more down-to-earth addresses: **Mario** on the Piazza delle Coppelle (closed Sunday, 20,000 lire) and **Gino** in Vicolo Rosini (closed Sunday, 20,000 lire) on the Piazza del Parlamento.

A Visit to the Vicar of Christ

The smallest state in the world, with more 'citizens' than the USA and the Soviet Union put together; 700 million Catholics take their orders from the Holy See. Visit to St Peter and the Vatican Museums.

Undergound A 'Ottaviano' (700m/765yds on foot), Tram 19 (500m/547yds), Bus 64 (convenient but 'Diebes-Bus' gennant Vorsicht!), 51, 81, 907, 991 (500m/547yds), 34, 46, 62, 65, 98, 808, 881, 982 (300m/328yds), 23, 34, 41 (300m/328yds). Taxi to 'Piazza San Pietro'.

It's hardly even big enough to show up on a map; the Pope's kingdom only takes up 517,997m^2 (one fifth of a square mile). But nowhere else in the world will you find such an enormous accumulation of treasures both religious and artistic. Let's check the opening times to start with. The Vatican Museums are open from October–June, 8.45am–1pm, from July–September, 8.45am–4pm, and are closed on Sunday with the exception of the last Sunday in the month (entrance free). St Peter's closes in winter at 6pm, in summer at 7pm. So it makes sense to visit the museums first and then the cathedral. This variation means going straight to the entrance of the **Musei Vaticani**. Taxi or bus 49 (to Piazza Risorgimente, then walk), 32, 51, 81, 492, 907, 991. Underground A 'Ottaviano' then walk.

The Colonnade at St Peter's

'My first walk through Rome took me to St Peter's, the enormous size and indescribable magnificence of which is certainly a source of wonder; however, it has the feeling more of an imperial palace than of a temple to the living God. No reverence stirred in my heart...' Such were the impressions of Dorothea Schlegel, a Catholic convert, in 1818. And her perceptions were cor-

rect, **St Peter's** is the pure embodiment of a claim to power, right from the very first basilica with its five transepts, consecrated in AD326. The Papal Altar, now with Bernini's High Baroque bronze canopy, was supposed to have been erected over the grave of the Apostle Peter. Pius XII wanted to know for sure and ordered excavations to be carried out, which continued in a highly disorderly fashion until 1949. The remains of the coffin and body of the Vicar of Christ ended up unrecognised in a store-room with other finds before finally being identified by the archaeologist Margherita Guarducci by the fragments of the imperial purple and gold cloth in which Constantine had wrapped Peter's corpse. The beams of the grave bear the imperial seal.

It is no longer possible to confirm whether the Basilica of Constantine was as hopelessly decayed in the 15th century as Pope Nicolas V maintained. The Renaissance was the herald of more than just a wave of building. Julius II, elected in 1504, saw himself as the second Julius Caesar and announced his intention of restoring the continuity between imperial and papal Rome by transforming the Vatican into an imperial Acropolis. To realise his plan, he needed a new St Peter's.

This gigantic project was too ambitious even for the finances of the church state. The sale of indulgences shot up throughout the Western world; the Protestant rhyme goes 'pennies in the priest's hand will save the souls in all the land'. 'Non olet'—money doesn't stink; Vespasian used to rake in money from the charges for using the public toilets, and Leo X followed in his footsteps by taxing whores. The horizontal profession brought in 20,000 ducats a year in aid of the basilica, more than came in from saving souls.

The House of God, intended as a demonstration of Rome's primacy over the whole of Christendom, was a major cause of schism. The Counter-Reformation had brought about a shift in ideological emphasis and a change of dimensions. It was no longer nostalgia for ancient times, but rather the desire to attack the new

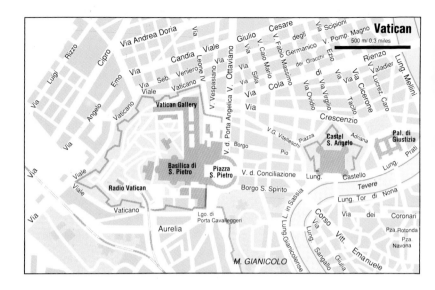

heresies which coloured the ideas of the Church's governors. The Council of Trent (1545–63) called for a spectacular Catholicism, a hierarchy with a place for everyone.

The Neo-Platonist ideal of a square central element (the earth) and a hemispherical dome (the heavens), united in the symbolical form of Christ's martyrdom, the cross, was no longer enough. Every architect from Bramante to Michelangelo had been fired with enthusiasm by this ideal form. However, it could not satisfy the demands of the Counter-Reformation, which aimed at fascinating the faithful, but also at regimenting them. St Peter's was redesigned as a basilica, 186m (612ft) long and 15,160m^2 (163,182 square feet) in area, with the capacity to hold 60,000 people. The Catholic Church of the Western world stayed unshakeably Roman. That's not such a bad idea, when you look at the north–south divide from an artistic point of view. You only have to look at the churches to see that Catholicism won hands down. 'There is nothing small here, even if some aspects deserve blame or are devoid of taste; everything shares in the greatness of the whole.' Goethe's words on Rome are especially apt in the case of St Peter's. Take Bernini's **colonnades**, symbolically embracing the city and the earth (the Pope's blessing is *'urbi et orbi'*). Here the details of the 140 saints, 284 pillars, 88 pilasters or the ellipse, 73m (720ft) in diameter, are not the most important thing. What is truly breathtaking is the sheer architectural spirit with which this church impresses itself upon the world.

The museum bus goes through the Arco delle Campane (belltower gate) between the sacristy and St Peters. On the left is the Vatican courthouse and the station, on the right the mosaic school and the palace of the governing body; on the left again the Eagle Fountain, eyes right for the Papal Academy of Science, look left for the

40

Chinese Pavilion, and finally the entrance to the museums, where 2 million visitors per year follow the 'trail' for around 7.24km (4½ miles). Four different routes are marked:

A (violet) takes around 1½ hours; Michelangelo in the Sistine Chapel and back; the rest isn't so important.

B (beige) three hours, adds on Etruscan, Roman, Early Christian and ethnological collections.

C (green) 3½ hours, with Egyptians, Romans, Raphael's Rooms, the Fra Angelico frescos, Appartamento Borgia with Pinturicchio and modern sacred art and the library.

D (yellow) five hours, takes in the lot.

We'll give ourselves the green light (route C), speed up at Modern Art (keep going), leave the library alone and take in the Pinacotheca instead. The official *Guide to the Vatican Museums and the Vatican City* (published by the Holy See, price 10,000 lire) is full of useful information. Follow the herd down the one-way track to the **Cortile della Pigna**, a courtyard with large antique bronze pine cones, then go left up the stairs before the glass door and turn right into the **Museo Egizio**, the Egyptian Museum.

Room 1: next to the column on the right is a Pharaoh who fits in very well here—Amenophis IV, Nefertiti's husband, also known as Echnaton, or 'the man the Sun God loves'. He was the first monotheist in history, even if he couldn't manage to assert his creed. His noble face and delicate hands, the elegant folds of his garment on the fragment of relief epitomise the harmony of Egyptian art. The sarcophagi are covered in colourful depictions of nature, from newts and snakes to gods with dogs', falcons' or lions' heads; there's a wide range of nature's children. This was no culture that demanded distance between Man and Nature ('subdue the earth . . . and have dominion over every living thing'), and the Egyptians seem to have felt thoroughly at home in it.

Room II: the mummy of a slip of a girl who was prepared for the afterlife by being given a henna rinse and a perm, a last reminder of the vanity of her sex.

But why go to all this trouble to preserve the dead? Because the Egyptians believed in the resurrection of the flesh, and took it as literally as the Christians who took up residence in the catacombs. To make sure that the big-wigs of Nile society kept the cushiness of their number in the afterlife, they took their household staff with them, plus a slave-driver with a whip for good measure. There they stand like tin soldiers, known as **Ushebti**

On watch in the Vatican: the Swiss Guard

(responders) because they had to cry 'here!' at roll-call.

Room III exhibits the Egypt which Hadrian had rebuilt in Tivoli. The beloved youth Antonius was drowned in the Nile on 30 October; in this tableau he is seen rising from the dead on a lotus bloom, to be deified as Antonius-Osiris. The Egyptians were aesthetes, the Assyrians were realists, and the crude relief scenes from Nineveh and Nimrod, blackened by the fire of the conquering troops, are a perfect example of this. Corpses floating in the Tigris; winged demons protecting the Tree of Life, the forerunners of our angels.

Go to the right now, up the steps and down the long corridor of the **Museo Chiaramonti**, with a wealth of gods and emperors created by the sculptor Antonio Canova—plus, under Number X on the ground, the miller P Nonius Zethus from Ostia. Right at the closed mesh grille and you'll find the **Bracchio Nuovo** (new wing), with Roman sculptures in a classicist setting (Raphael Stern, 1820), a collage of heroes.

In the fourth niche on the right is the Prima Porta *Augustus* (named after his place of excavation), in oratorical pose and wearing a breastplate with hours of stories shown on it in relief; 'I forced the Parthians to give back the spoils and insignia of three Roman armies and to beg for the friendship of the Roman people', dictated the emperor. And the gods rejoiced as well—a whole troop of them were delighted to see peace. The Lord of the earth is barefoot, because heroes don't wear shoes. And his stance has been copied from Polycletes' *Doryphoros* (javelin thrower, diagonally opposite). The peacocks in gold bronze come from Hadrian's villa, and the colossal Nile complete with crocodile, sphinx and idyllic scene in relief (1st century AD) once stood behind the Pantheon.

Back to the Egyptians, but this time go past them and straight on to the **Museo Pio-Clementino**. The *Vestibolo Quadrato* leads you to the *Gabinetto dell Apoxyomenes* (the strigil user or scraper), a copy of Lysippus' figure of an athlete scraping the sweat from his body after a race. No strutting victor this, but one who shows the ravages of his efforts. On the left is the Cortile Ottagono with the *Belvedere Apollo*.

Winckelmann, that guru of classicism, once wrote: 'The statue of Apollo is the highest artistic ideal among all the ancient works of sculpture which escaped destruc-

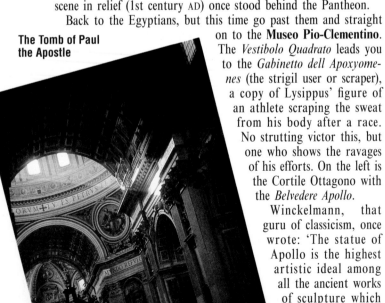

The Tomb of Paul the Apostle

tion.' Superlatives like that always induce a feeling of speechlessness, dependent as they are on the time in which they are formulated, and possibly even—this statue depicts an attractive youth—on the hormones of the speaker. The marble copy dates from Imperial times; the bronze original by Leochares (330BC) once stood in the Agora in Athens. Apollo, the avenging 'sharp-shooter', would make you think nowadays of a rocket-launcher, but in those times the god's outstretched hand held a bow and arrow.

The Apolline principle as the symbol of pure spirituality: 'Thus the gods decree that poor mortals shall live in woe while themselves remaining untouched by all sorrow', wrote Homer in the *Iliad*, and that takes us neatly to the next corner and to the Trojan priest *Laocoon*, who warned his people of the horse which the Greeks had left as a 'votive offering for Athene'. The spear he hurled at the treacherous animal enraged the goddess, who promptly set a horde of sea-serpents on him and his sons. The Laocoon group, the work of the Rhodian sculptors Hagesandros, Athanodoros and Polydoros, portrays this unfair divine persecution, which only Aeneas managed to survive.

On to the **Sala degli Animali**, the biggest marble zoo of the ancient world. The right-hand wing contains Mithras the Persian God of Light, killing the Bull, symbol of fertility, from whose blood Creation arose; the scorpion and snake attempt to prevent this as evil spirits, the dog licks up the blood. The conflict between light and darkness, good and evil fascinated Roman legionaries, and the mystery cult, which also included a ceremony of baptism, was to be found everywhere in the Empire as far afield as Hadrian's Wall. Divinity, which we encounter even more often, is the guardian of truth and fidelity among men.

From the right-hand wing of the menagerie, pass into the **Galleria delle Statue**. On the left in the niche you'll see *Ariadne Sleeping*—in the past confused with Cleopatra; on the right is the

Pilgrim musicians

Eros of Centocelle. At the back on the right is the **Galleria dei Busti**, and to the right of the window the Knidian Venus, a copy of the cult statue by Praxiteles in the sacred shrine of Knidos. For the first time in her history, the goddess of love is depicted naked, apparently believing that she is alone. Rather like Susanna and the elders, except that here the voyeurs are not dirty old men, but visitors to the museum.

Back through the Sala degli Animali to the **Sala della Muse**. In the centre is the *Torso of Belvedere*, who to judge from the lion-skin is Hercules. 'Appolonius of Athens, son of Nestor, created him', according to the signature on the stone (1st century BC). Michelangelo fell into raptures at the sight of the giant; 'Truly, its creator was a man who is wiser than nature itself! How tragic that it is only a torso!' Which could go a long way towards explaining those muscle-bound forms in the Sistine Chapel. In the **Sala Rotunda** we meet Hadrian's *Antonius* among the bodybuilders. The gold bronze Hercules from the Pompeian theatre suffered a curious fate; he was struck by lightning, promptly buried with full honours and only came to light again in 1864.

Back in the **Sala a Croce Greca**, where we started with the Egyptians; on the left is the sarcophagus of red porphyry, which is attributed to Constantine's pious mother Helena, although its war-like motifs don't really suit her. It shows victorious Romans enslaving humiliated barbarians. On the right, the sarcophagus of Constantine's daughter Constantia displays winged figures called Eroti engaged in harvesting grapes and making wine; Christian or Dionysian? Both cultures contain myths of wine being transformed into divine blood. Up the steps and straight on for the long trek to Raphael's Rooms (the Etruscan Museum on the left at the top is only open on Monday, Tuesday, Thursday and Friday) which takes you through the Galleria dei Candelabri, degli Arazzi, delle Carte Geografiche, Sale Sobieski and dell' Immacolata and into the **Sala**

di Constantino, decorated with battle scenes by Raphael's pupils. Left through the Sala dei Chiaroscuri into the **Cappella Niccolina**, to the graceful frescos of Fra Angelico, the master of the early Renaissance, which show scenes from the life of St Stephen (upper section) and St Laurence (lower section). Then go back through the Constantine Room and into the **Stanza di Eliodoro**, painted by Raphael in 1514. Take a moment's rest on the bench at the window.

The museum directors have presented Raphael back to front so that the stream of visitors flows more evenly; the first picture you see, *Heliodoros Driven Out of the Temple in Jerusalem* (1514), is actually the final picture in the cycle. It represents a crucial point in the history of art; for the Renaissance sought those who centred their lives around their own inner harmony. The middle of this picture is empty, as if the Big Bang had just taken place. But the crowd pursuing the robber almost bursts out of the frame. Frenzy shows clearly in the faces of the persecutors. A new era—that of mannerism and early baroque—is undergoing a stormy birth, and this genius was the first to feel it.

Raphael lets his employer Julius II (left) watch Heliodoros' crash-landing with every appearance of enjoyment; after all, the miscreant has to suffer on behalf of all unlawful occupiers of church state property. Julius is also depicted as St Peter asleep, over the window in the centre, and then freed by the angel, over on the right, while the guards raise the alarm on the left. Julius kneels before the altar in the *Bolsena Mass*, when blood drips from the Host, demonstrating the presence of Christ. And he even plays a dual role in *Leo the Great meeting Attila*; when the fresco was begun he was still a cardinal, but by the end he was Pope, so Raphael portrayed him twice over.

A personality cult? Certainly; Raphael was a courtier, so to speak, which in those days was not seen as servility, but as honour. He had his painting school, which means that in these rooms you can never be sure where the maestro put down the brush and where his pupils picked it up. The brown-spotted horse in the Attila picture probably got a cow-skin painted on it by mistake—only a beginner could be that stupid, according to popular belief. Raphael loved wine, women and song, and enjoyed a closer relationship with the Pope than 'that clod Michelangelo'.

The atmosphere is somewhat rarefied in heaven, both in Dante's *Divine Comedy*, where hell is much more exciting, and in Raphael's *Stanza della Segnatura*. In the *Disputa* the holiest representatives of Heaven and earth are assembled in two semicircles, for the purpose—according to the German author Thoma and his *Munich Man In Heaven*—of warbling ecstatic choruses of Halleluja and scoffing manna. Of course Julius, the party smartie, is in the picture too. Apollo is playing the fiddle in *Parnassus*, but the collection of poets there, including Dante, look as bored as if they were at a Pink Floyd concert waiting for the band to come on.

The *School of Athens* as the Valhalla of mortal philosophy—Raphael's vision of St Peter's-to-be—is the most powerful work of the collection. Plato, with the features of Leonardo da Vinci, and Aristotle are truly divine: one pointing upwards as an idealist, the other holding his hand between here and there, weighing up the two directions. The two facets of human thought fulfil the middle way; in them is the origin of all movement.

The ancient world, said Raphael, is a perfect model, a gift from Providence. Art has the task of spreading the beauty of nature and history among the people. God reveals himself fully in Man and in all creation, and the artist's highest ideal must be to emulate the beauty of God's works. *La bellezza* is truer than truth, more lifelike than life itself—a reality which is yet above the things of reality. And thus there is no point in merely painting a copy of these things; the artist must collect the fragments of beauty in existence in the world. One picture has such fullness, such density, that it is without equal. No wonder that the artists themselves are there at such a momentous event. Raphael, second from the left, looks searchingly out of the 'School', next to him his pupil Sodoma. On Plato's left are Socrates, Alcibiades and Alexander the Great, the last in armour.

The drop-out lounging around on the steps is Diogenes, and the life-style guru on the left by the remains of the column is Epicurus with his crown of vine leaves. Averroës the Arab is looking over Pythagoras' shoulder as the latter is doing his calculations, and

In the Sistine Chapel

The creation of man

Heraclitus, propped up on his elbow, is a homage to Michelangelo. The bald man with the compasses is Euclid, alias Bramante.

In the *Fire in Borgo* (the quarter around St Peter's) Leo X can be seen on the Benediction Loggia of the old Basilica of Constantine; the melodramatic panic of the crowd is reminiscent of a Verdi opera. From here, all roads lead to the **Sistine Chapel**, through the Borgia Chambers painted by Pinturicchio, where the collection of modern religious art is exhibited under lighting which can blind you as you try to look at the frescoes. In the chapel itself, however, the light can be turned off altogether in good weather. The story of the Creation covering the ceiling exudes its own radiance thanks to the latest clean-up operation, which removed the soot and grime of centuries, revealing Michelangelo's original blazing colours and rendering 28,000 Watts completely superfluous.

A revolutionary act, because art historians had built up a whole metaphysical world around that layer of dirt. Michelangelo, lover of darkness, a 'painter of melancholy and of sin'; Eckart Peterich, that guru on all matters Italian, wrote of the prophets and sibyls ranged around the outside, 'A desolate world of shadows; they live as if in other-worldly caves...' Michelangelo saw himself as a sculptor. 'The closer painting comes to relief work, the better I find it', was his opinion, and the emphasis on the physicality of his 343 heroes provides visual proof. Only the pressure brought to bear on him by Julius II made him paint at all. The relationship was stormy on both sides. Julius II wanted the ceiling to represent the *Twelve Apostles*, which the artist maintained was 'a poor subject'. 'Why?' asked the Pope. 'Because apostles are always poor', was the answer. 'Do what you like, then!' cried Julius II angrily. And Michelangelo did. But he never ceased to complain; 'painting is to sculpture as the darkness is to the light of understanding.'

From 1508 Michelangelo painted for four long years; 'my loins are slipping deep into my belly, my rump is rolled up as a cushion.' After only a few weeks he sent away the assistants he had hired, unable to tolerate anyone else. He unrolled Genesis from the end

Whither?

to the beginning, from Judith and Holofernes to 'Let there be light!' At first he changed a great deal, but soon corrections became rarer and rarer. There's no doubt that a genius is at work, overshadowing Perugino, Botticelli, Ghirlandaio, Rosselli, Pinturicchio, Signorelli, all the previous painters of the chapel walls. But Michelangelo was also a fine craftsman; the plastering and technique used in the Sistine Chapel are so perfect that they have even survived a badly leaking roof. Michelangelo immersed himself in the art of the ancients with the viewpoint of a Christian; a perfect model the ancient world may have been, but with the revelation of divine truth in mind, the artist had to progress beyond the model. The eternally incomplete, the tension of the soul fixed on a distant, unattainable divinity—that, for him, was art.

Christ's arrogant gesture in the *Day of Judgement* (1541), which shatters the universe, hurls the damned into the Inferno even as they stammer with fear over their fate, and transports the saved, transfigured, into the Kingdom of Heaven, is the key to this awe of God. Once more Michelangelo had demonstrated that he was no mere official artist of a regime, for his vision of the *Day of Wrath* got so many backs up among the Counter-Reformers that three Popes seriously considered having the whole lot knocked down again. Christ doesn't have a beard, the angels have no wings, the saints have no haloes, and to crown it all there's that heathen Charon, ferryman of the dead; all these transgressions against the rules of pictorial art were grounds for strong protest. After all, how are you supposed to tell the difference between angels without wings and devils, or saints without haloes and damned souls?

Christ is naked, as is Saint Catherine of Alexandria; who is lying on her front, so Saint Biagio can get an immodest eyeful. And then there are all those other naked figures! 'Your work belongs in a gorgeous bathroom, but not in a church choir', spluttered Pietro Aretino, who had himself published the first illustrated sex education book with Giulio Romano, a pupil of Raphael's. Daniele da Volterra, the 'painter of trousers', set to work, and St Biagio had his head turned—towards Christ. Michelangelo, who had immortalised himself as the prophet Jeremiah and in the broken body of St Bartholomew, was cut down to size. At the moment, the *Last Judgement* is under wraps for restoration.

The way out is down the long corridor and past the library. Just in case you still have the energy to take a quick peep into the **Pinacotheca** (picture gallery), you'll find many great names. The fresco fragments by Melozzo di Forli (*Angels Making Music*) are a special treat, and you should definitely slow down for the Raphael Room. *The Ascension of Christ*, the maestro's last picture (1520), spans the whole gamut of emotions.

Ordinary mortals will be feeling a bit hungry after this artistic marathon. The self-service restaurant by the Pinacotheca is useful if you're pushed for time, but if you want to eat in more civilised surroundings, try **La Rondinella**, Via Vespasiano 25 (Piazza Risorgimento, closed Sunday, 25,000 lire) and **La Mejo Pastaciutta**, Piazza Risorgimento 5 (closed Monday, 30,000 lire): From there you can walk to St Peter's. If you don't mind a bus ride: **Tre Pupazzi**, Borgo Pio 183 (closed Sunday, 30,000 lire).

Back to the basilica. In the entrance hall on the right (behind the glass door) you'll find Bernini's statue of Constantine on horseback, and on the left is Cornacchini's *Charlemagne* (18th century). Of the five portals, the ones by Filarete from Old St Peter's (in the middle, including Christ, Mary, the martyrdom of Peter and Paul) and Manzu's *Porta della Morte* (1964, outside on the left) are the most significant. In the basilica itself on the right is Michelangelo's only signed work, his *Pietà*. Any book will tell you it's a masterpiece,

Guilty conscience

49

the more so because he was only 23 when he completed it in 1498. But it isn't quite that simple to sum up Michelangelo's art. Look into the mother's face. She is holding her dead son on her lap, yet she seems to have some inner serenity, her expression, seen from close-to, is one of calmness, although any normal 'Mamma' in that situation would be sobbing with pain. Christ's body still bears the sweat of death. But she not only has perfectly dry eyes, she is also younger than Jesus.

These contradictions were pointed out to Michelangelo by his contemporaries. He answered Ascanio Condivi by saying 'Didn't you know that chaste women stay young far longer than the unchaste? So how much younger must a virgin stay whose mind has never known the slightest lustful thought which might have eaten away at her body?' Rubbish, and especially so in Rome, where there are hordes of nuns who appear to age in exactly the same way as married women. Could it be, to draw malicious conclusions, that they're just as 'unchaste' as any others? No, the reason is that Michelangelo's view of the planet Venus was a rather distorted one. All the women in his version of the Creation are androgynous and it is rumoured that he never saw a naked woman in his life.

Every fold of Mary's robe expresses the mother's despair and the artist's genius, according to authorities on the subject. But just take a closer look. That robe isn't so unusual; think of the fashions of the last few years, where women have taken to wearing such heavily padded shoulders that they all look like Brunhilde. Italian art historians have a more plausible explanation of the enormous amount of care lavished on the robe: the young Michelangelo simply wanted to demonstrate to his employers how expertly he could carve flesh and flowing robes out of marble.

Further down the right-hand aisle, pass the memorial to Christina of Sweden, a convert to Catholicism, on the left; the inscription dubs her 'Queen of the Goths and Vandals'. On the right, Francesco Messina's hard, inquisitorial Pius XII. St Peter is as the basilica of 'representation and of triumph' is borne out everywhere. Even the pictures are mosaic enlargements—the only original is Pietro da Cortona's *Holy Trinity* in the **Sacramental Chapel** (the tabernacle in the form of Bramante's temple of St Pietro in Montorio, the two golden angels are by Bernini).

Popes don't fall into anonymity when they die, they're enthroned on high as colossi, gesturing in a way which combines a blessing and a command. At their feet their virtues are spread out as allegories—Canova made what was more or less a Statue of Liberty for Clemens XIII. Eros and Thanatos, the buxom woman and Death with the clepsydra, are on Bernini's tombs of Urban VIII and Alexander VII; 'Everyman' in St Peter's.

Bernini as the master of ghost trains and light shows; his angels in the apse attract light like a magnet. In the centre the Holy Ghost is seen descending in the form of a dove. The *Cathedra Petri* (below), the throne flanked by the Fathers of the Church, Ambrosius and Augustinus (front), Athanasius and Johannes Chrysostomos, was said to contain the seat from which Peter preached. When it was opened in 1970 the mediaeval grave of Charles the Bald was found. But on the other hand, the bronze *Peter on the Throne* (under the right-hand central pillar), which was attributed to Arnolfo di Cambio (around 1300), was discovered to date back to ancient times. The toes are polished clean from being kissed and touched. Keep to the right and return to the lift which takes you up to the terrace; you'll have to cover the last 45m (150ft) up to the dome (total 119m/390ft) on foot (open 8am–4.45pm; summer 8am–6.15pm). An alternative to scaling the heights of the dome would be to descend to the depths of the grottoes with the Papal graves (open 7am–5.30pm; summer till 6pm) and visit the treasury (open 9am–12.30pm; 3–4.30pm; summer 3–6.30pm).

Finally, here are some tips for dinner in the neighbourhood: in **Tre Archi** (Via Coronari 233, 25,000 lire) Giacchino, the landlord, serves hearty Roman food. If you want to end the day in more spiritual company, nuns of the Order of Les Travailleuses-Missionaires run **L'Eau Vive** (Via Monterone 85a, near the Pantheon, 60,000 lire). Monsignori and Christian Democrats come here to eat gourmet French food and, now and again, to strike up a heavenly chorus of *Ave Maria*.

Pick & Choose

1. The Archaic Smile

From the Etruscans to Arte Moderna: 3,000 years of art in two extraordinary museums behind Pincio. Morning tour.

Tram: 19, 29N; underground A 'Flaminio'; taxi 'Museo Etrusco Villa Giulia'

This morning is a dialectic because it is going to try and unite opposites: the Etruscans in the **Museo Nazionale di Villa Giulia** (9am–7pm, Sunday 9am–1pm, closed Monday) and the **Galleria Nazionale d'Arte Moderna** (9am–2pm, Sunday 9am–1pm, closed Monday).

The Flaminio underground station is on the **Piazza del Popolo**. Go through the gate and stop for breakfast at **Rosati** (on the right). Walk to the **Pincio** and cross the bridge into **Villa Borghese Park** (keeping the platform at your back), turn left at the big fountain and continue in the same direction. A huge flight of steps will lead you to **Viale delle Belle Arti**, where you can already see the Arte Moderna gallery; round the curve to the left and you're at the villa of the last Pope of the Renaissance, Julius III (1551–3).

The Etruscans received guests in the same position as they

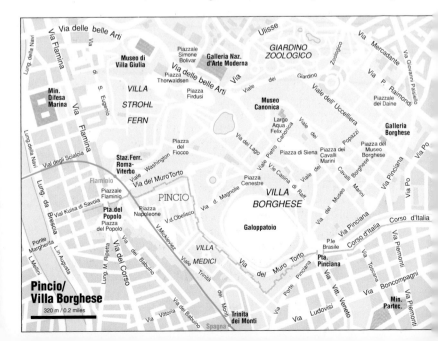

Smiling Etruscans

adopted for eating—reclining, the head propped up on one hand. And they do that on their coffins too; after all, eating good food is one of the greatest pleasures, and the Etruscans expected to get their due ration of the good life in the hereafter. You may not be able to take it with you, or so people think nowadays, but the Etruscans tried very hard; there they are with all their luggage, on resurrection standby. The grave as a paean to the delights of home life and everyday pleasures—that's what makes us feel so close to the Etruscans. The slant-eyed centaur (about 1000BC) at the entrance used to have the task of frightening evil spirits away from the dead; today his job is enticing visitors into the museum.

The first things you see are assorted objects forged from metal—safety-pins, razors, tools, keys and locks. The Etruscans were master metal-workers, and their gold jewellery, in either filigree or granular technique, is among the most beautiful in the ancient world. And one thing which is particularly striking about this domestic idyll is that any primitive stage of vacillation is absent. Everything, down to vases and crockery, has that perfection of form which, in utensils, comes from the perfect balance of form and function. What has our consumer society got to offer to compete with such perfection?

But the real link between the Etruscans and the art of today was their preference for the 'poor' materials of *arte povera*: wood, tufa stone, terracotta. Greek temples had to be of marble, like the divinities they worshipped; Etruscans were content with earthenware, that warm, magic substance. The unearthly beauty of the *Apollo of Vejo*, in a delicately flowing robe, is entrancing. He fought Hercules, who had killed a deer sacred to him, high up on a ridge; Vulca, the only Etruscan artist whose name has been handed down to us, proportioned his figures using the perspective of a spectator down below. The archaic smile may express both merriment and despair (after the Irpinia earthquake in 1980, people who pain had rendered speechless wore this smile). But the married couple attending a feast on the clay sarcophagus (6th century) exude well-being from every pore. Only the Etruscans acknowledged equality between men and women—among the Romans and Greeks, only courtesans were allowed to attend public events. He lays one arm tenderly around the shoulders of his delicate-fingered wife, dressed up as if for a fashion show with pointed shoes, an elegant tunic and brimless hat—all befitting her station. Her version of the archaic smile has a mischievous twinkle. A fifth-century war chariot—not only the hero believed in the gods, the horses had to as well. It's like a Catholic pilgrimage church; there are arms, hands and heads of clay, but also breasts, wombs and internal organs.

Where did the Etruscans come from? They're certainly not Indo-Germanic. There were two theories in the ancient world, which experts are still fighting over today. They may have been the original inhabitants of Italy (their own belief) driven out by waves of Indo-Germanic immigrants—Latins, Greeks and Gauls. Alternatively, they may have been immigrants from Asia Minor. An intimate form of art, then, and the reason for the Etruscans ending up in such a small setting as the Villa Giulia with its painted vines, animals, *putti* and the splashing of the Nymphaeum to round it off. The Renaissance was none too keen on all that flexing of Imperial muscle either, and the sculptor Marino Marini and the painter Massimo Campigli, who we're off to visit in the Galleria d'Arte Moderna (274m/300yds along on the right) announced *unisono*, *'Ich bin ein Etruscan'*.

'Modern'—a word you can stretch like a piece of chewing-gum. Rome's Temple of the Muses dates from the period of industrial expansion (1911), and actually opens with Canova, the genius with marble (1757–1822), which is funny because modern is the last word you'd apply to him—he has all the hot-house lasciviousness of an upper-class salon. So the menu opens with soupy schmaltz, and pure hamming. But there are some real treats—Klimt, Courbet, van Gogh, Cézanne. The Italians occupy most of the space, some of them also famous beyond their own borders—Macchaioli, the Futurists, the Roman School. A fascinating record of art which rebelled against tradition but never quite managed to shake off the light and shade of the past.

2. The Prince's Park

Stroll through a stupendous collection of artistic treasures and enjoy a taste of the dolce vita; through the park of the Villa Borghese to the Via Veneto. Afternoon tour.

Underground A and Rapid Transit Roma North 'Flaminio'; bus 2, 90, 95, 115, 119, 202, 204, 490, 495; tram 225; taxi 'Piazza del Popolo'.

The focal point of the **Piazza del Popolo** is the **obelisk**, set up by Rameses 3,200 years ago before the sun god's shrine in Heliopolis; then brought to the Circus Maximus by Augustus 2,000 years ago; finally, the architect Giuseppe Valadier used it as the focal point of this square, encircled by baroque and classicist architecture. In the reign of Napoleon, obelisks were cult objects. The emperor, who had declared Rome to be his second capital, wanted to leave only magnificence behind him and thus set the court architect Berthault by the side of Valadier. After the Corsican was ousted, the dimensions were toned down and a kind of open-air salon was created, harmonious and—thanks to the exclusion of traffic—peaceful.

At the domes of S **Maria di Montesanto** (1675) and S **Maria dei Miracoli** (1679, built by Rinaldi, Bernini and Fontana) begins the **Tridente**, as the Romans call the Vie di Ripetta, del Corso and del Babuino. Opposite on the right is S **Maria del Popolo**, with a little dome, a twin of which—long live symmetry—was promptly slapped onto the barracks of the Carabinieri on the other side for good measure.

The Temple of Aesculapius in the Villa Borghese

Winckelmann, Piranesi, Canova, David, Thorwaldsen, Valadier: Rome was the natural breeding-ground of European classicism, and the **Piazza del Popolo** is its most significant legacy in the city. The lower fountain down towards the Pincio depicts Rome (with she-wolf) between the Tiber and the Aniene. Let's climb up, keeping to the right, and enter the **Casino Valadier**, from which we see all Rome spread out before us (again).

Back to the observation platform, past the carousel to the **Fountain of Moses**; drink in the view of St Peter's dome, set off to perfection by the lush Mediterranean vegetation, a sight of rare beauty. Now head for the romantic **water-clock** of the Dominican father Giambattista Embriaco (1867). Over the bridge—you can see the *galoppatoio* for the horses to the right—the real **park** of the Villa Borghese begins. Like all great Roman families, the Borghese princes belonged to the 'black' nobility, that is, created by the Pope. For centuries these families supplied cardinals and many a successor to Peter as Vicar of Christ; amidst an impoverished population (for the church state's economic policies were usually pretty amateurish) these artistically minded gentlemen built themselves gorgeous residences. It was the norm to have a palazzo in the city and a villa in extensive parklands on the outskirts.

When Rome became the capital of Italy in 1870, an unprecedented bout of building mania broke out. Most of the aristocratic families stuck it out on their estates while speculators prowled over the land all around. The result was that Rome's only islands of green are the villas. In 1901 the Borghese was bought by the council, and is nowadays a paradise for children, skateboarders, joggers, cyclists, dogs and horses.

Straight on down the **Vialle delle Magnolie** to the **Rondello**. On the right at the top children can have fun riding on ponies and carousels, and there's a train (with rubber wheels) for a trip around the park. On the left is the stadium of the **Piazza di**

56

Siena, where all the big showjumping and racing events are held. Opposite is the **Giardino del Lago**, with the **Temple of Aesculapius** as a classic piece of showmanship on the island in the lake. Back on the street, the eye-catching ruins of the **Temple of Faustina** are a product of 'ruin romanticism'. Before you get there, on the left there's a quaint donkey with a cannon on its back and an alpino by its side: **la fortezzuola**, the little fortress in which the sculptor Pietro Canonica used to manufacture state monuments. Once upon a time you might have dismissed it as 'Kitsch!' Nowadays a more lenient view is taken of art, and it's possible to find the whole thing amusing, especially since the man really could produce attractive sculptures (open 9am–1.30pm, 3–7pm).

Through the 'Valley of the Dogs' to the **Villa Borghese** itself. Go round the building (swathed in scaffolding) to the left; the entrance is behind a builders' fence. There would have been far more to see in the exhibition of works of art if Napoleon hadn't helped himself so liberally for the Louvre. Mostly Bernini. Every time he stood in front of a block of rough marble, the master of creation must have vowed 'Let it be flesh!' His Daphne, with hands and feet turning into laurel branches as Apollo rescues her from violation, vibrates between terror and the last remnants of ecstasy.

Another fairly famous lady, Paolina Bonaparte-Borghese, the emperor's sister is also here. At first it's hard to know what to make of the *Venus Victorious*. Classic features like dozens of others, perfect, swelling maidenly breasts, faultless body. 'As cold as a lump of ice' found Italian critics, which may be true. R Zeitler wrote in *Notes on Casanova's Relationship to Women* that the sculptor had no sexual relationships with women. And what doesn't happen in the head can't happen in the senses, much less in marble. The **Via Veneto**, scene of Federico Fellini's *Dolce Vita*, is 457m (500yds) further on. Sit down in **Doney** or **Caffè de Paris** and dream a little—the myth has vanished, has fled looking for a new home.

3. The Divine Puzzle

In times of turbulence, Rome's master mosaic artists created beautiful puzzles. S Pudenziana, S Prassede and S Maria Maggiore are windows onto heaven. Morning tour.

Underground A and B 'Termini', Underground A 'Repubblica', walk to the Museo Nazionale Romano. Taxi to 'Museo delle Terme'.

Blowing your own trumpet is all part of business success, even if that business is religious belief. The consul Junius Bassus built a basilica on the Esquiline in 331 which was a testimony in stone to Neo-Pythagorean and Neo-Platonic ideas and was to defend paganism against Christianity. Christianity's retort was to spread propaganda in the form of church mosaics. In **Diocletian's Thermae** (open 9am–2pm, Sunday 9am–1pm, closed Monday), we enter an age which sought God with passion.

The museum is actually rather like an ancient elephants' graveyard, with marble fragments and pieces everywhere, crumbling away in the courtyards under the acid rain. The two newly opened exhibition halls, however, more than make up for that—restored works, not many of them, but all first class. Next door there are two examples of intarsio from the heroic basilica already mentioned, made from polychromatic glass, marble, semi-precious stones and mother-of-pearl, and in the same brilliant colours that Michelangelo used in the Sistine. A circus scene with the obese sponsor and four victors in the horse-race, spontaneously and vibrantly effective. The horses are still snorting with the effort of the race. Then three nymphs (the Virtues), carrying off the youth Hylas to lead him to a carefree, immortal existence. For, according to the underlying motif of the Bassus monument, the soul is immortal and transcendent.

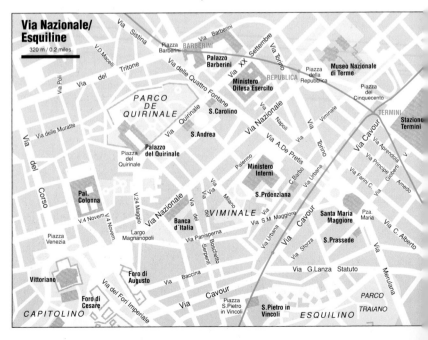

Via Nazionale/Esquiline

320 m / 0.2 miles

The Chapel of St Zeno in the basilica of S Prassedo

Both pagans and Christians believed in one God, and because of this similarity the battle between them was fierce. For Plotinus, the pioneer of Neo-Platonism, thought is movement, is the will to understand. To understand God it is necessary to open oneself to such an extent that one could become a god oneself. This state is a state of grace, is a gift from infinity, which allows the finite to merge with it.

The philosopher Wilhelm Windelbrand wrote that 'Christianity was only able to conquer the world of antique culture by absorbing and digesting it'. And Neo-Platonists too, who believed that the body and the sensuousness which originated in it were the prison of the spirit and the root of all evil, have left their traces in Christian thinking. What was it that the Devil presented to St Benedict or St Anthony when he wanted to lead them into temptation? Naked women, that's what, the ones like the torsos in the Thermae museum, with robes that reveal rather than conceal. And what else was the hermaphrodite, with girlish bottom and breasts, than pure provocation by lascivious nature? Every naked woman is the devil. Or rather, since they're all naked under their clothes, every woman is the devil.

As we proceed down the Via Cavour to S **Pudenziana** (via Urbana, 9am–12.30pm, 3–6pm), let's consider the consequences: Plotinus, who sought direct communication with God, was an enemy of the Church, because he needed neither Christ and the Revelation nor the intervention of Peter's successors and their hierarchy. The Fathers of the Church helped to beat down paganism in sowing the seed of mediaeval scholasticism, but the problem still existed. Neo-Platonism is an evergreen, and put out shoots not only in the Renaissance but also in Christian mysticism. When John Paul II warns the faithful against unauthorised moral judgements and admonishes that the way to heaven lies in the office church, he is speaking on the same ideological level as the mosaics.

The Paradise in the apse of S Pudenziana is no place for Joe Bloggs; it is intended for the initiated. Christ sits in the centre, but not as an anguished figure most normal stress-plagued mortals can identify with; here, he is Caesar. And the cross is no longer a symbol of passion here. The *crux gemmata*, made of gold inlaid with precious stones, is the sign of power. Two women—probably Pudenziana and Praxedis, but possibly also personifications of paganism and Judaism—hand him the victor's laurel wreath. The assembly of Apostles is dressed in noble senatorial garb, and behind a porticus, the temples and palaces of the Heavenly Jerusalem unfurl into the distance. The four science-fiction figures of the Apocalypse, the symbols of the Four Evangelists, sweep down from the sky. This picture-book, going back to the end of the fourth century, already contains some themes we'll see in later works.

Pudenziana and Praxedis were the daughters of Senator Prudens, who is said to have given Peter shelter. In the mornings, you can take a guided tour of the living-quarters, with floors from various centuries, and of the street in front—the sewage system works as well today as ever it did. A flight of steps in the yard takes you to a chapel on the second floor, with frescos from the year 1000, another version of the two martyrs handing Christ the laurel wreath, with the covered hands demanded of Byzantine court etiquette in dealings with the emperor. This tradition also delivered the arrangement of figures—standing next to each other, with no background. However, the daughters are no mere ciphers; they're living characters. And this in turn places them within Roman (western) culture, which never lost sight of the individual. Byzantine influences never quite took hold on the Tiber, because of the strong sense of local identity. The Christ in the mosaics is also no Pantocrator on a pedestal, but an affable ruler holding an audience with an animated group of his subjects.

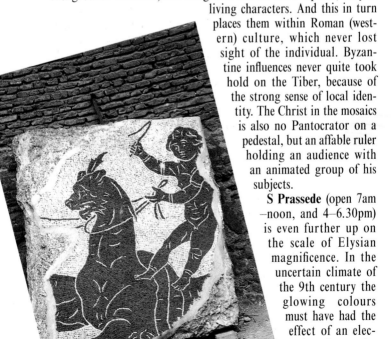

S Prassede (open 7am –noon, and 4–6.30pm) is even further up on the scale of Elysian magnificence. In the uncertain climate of the 9th century the glowing colours must have had the effect of an electric fire; the faithful emerged from the darkness to warm his shivering bones at the parable of eternal life in high style—then it was back into the chill of everyday life again. Once again we see the *Heavenly Jerusalem*, its gem-studded portals guarded by archangels, on the triumphal arch between the choir and the nave. Christ rules in the centre, followed by two angels, John the Baptist, the apostles, Elias, Moses and a band of saints marching into the eternal and heavenly city.

Artistic metaphors in an attempt to leave the earth behind, but which are forced to employ earthly images: the arch of the apse features the Apocalyptic Lamb, the book with seven seals, the seven candles, left and right—with the perspective leading towards the figure of Christ in the apse—the 24 white-robed elders of the apocalypse bringing the Lamb of God the gold wreaths which once the emperor of Rome received from his provinces. And, finally, fortissimo, the redeemer on a cloud—not a real cloud, just the idea of one. This universe is complete and perfect—there is no wind in Heaven, there are no clouds. On one side Peter is seen leading Pudentiana and Zeno to Christ, on the other Paul leads Praxedis and Pabst Paschalis, who has the square blue halo of the living. But not only the Pontifex has his ordained place in the events of salvation; the emperor too is superelevated by the appearance of Christ with the insignia of power. The Pope and the emperor, we are to believe, already have their places in the land flowing with milk and honey.

A class-ridden society, as Heine said, 'a lullaby from heaven for the idiots on earth'? That too. The colours and the stylised figures are bewitchingly beautiful and refreshing. In the Chapel of **St Zeno**, dating from Carolingian times, the angels are bedizened with expressionistic rouge and lipstick—the master of the 'Tiber Dionysus' from the Thermae Museum achieved the effect of make-up on the bronzes by using copper, with the eyes picked out in ivory.

The *Coronation of Mary* from the late 13th century, the work of the Franciscan monk Jacopo Torriti, is the last station on our expedition through the mosaics, to be found in **S Maria Maggiore** (open 7am–7pm). Under the windows of the nave are 36 scenes in the narrative style of book illustrations, depicting Old Testament elements and dating back to the time of Sixtus III, the church's builder. He ordered the basilica to be built after a miraculous fall of snow on 5 August, 352. The triumphal arch is sadly only illuminated sufficiently during services; it shows scenes from Christ's childhood, with changing effects of colour and light that seem to give a premonition of Impressionism.

4. Fashion City

Rome as the seat of fashion. A shopping stroll from the Piazza di Spagna. Afternoon.

Underground A 'Spagna'; bus 114; taxi 'Caffè Greco, Via Condotti'.

Everything is interconnected, the concept of fashion and the changing fashions themselves, seeing and being seen, the theatre of the **Piazza di Spagna** and the catwalk of the **Corso**. Before we start on our stroll, let's pause a moment in **Antico Caffè Greco** (Via Condotti), which according to one of its regulars, King Ludwig I of Bavaria, should have been renamed 'Caffè Tedesco', because all the 'northern lights' from Goethe downhill had gone there. 'Terrible people, when you watch them sitting in their old Caffè Greco', mocked Felix Mendelssohn-Bartholdy, the composer, in 1830. In those days the Empire-style cosiness and the romantic wall-tableaux of the ancient world had not yet been introduced; 'a small, dark room about eight paces wide; smoking tobacco is permitted only on one side of the chamber, and not on the other.'

The composer-cum-fashion reporter continued, 'the Germans sit upon the benches with wide hats upon their heads, great butchers' dogs at their sides, and their necks, cheeks, indeed their entire faces covered with hair; they produce quantities of smoke (only on one side of the chamber), tell each other coarse anecdotes; their dogs promulgate vermin; a kneckerchief or a cutaway would be improvements—any area of the face not covered by the beard is covered by the spectacles...' And these were pious artists, the Nazarenes, in fact, who Mendelssohn was poking fun at; 'they drink their coffee and talk of Titian and Pordenone as if these last were sitting next to them, clad like themselves in beards and wide brims! And then they produce such sickly Madonnas, feeble saints,

The busy Spanish Steps

milksops of heroes that sometimes one is gripped by the
urge to violence...'

The philosopher Arthur
Schopenhauer also had a run-
in with the Nazarenes, basically an up-to-date version
of the old pagan-Christian
battle, for he advised the
painters to take the
Greek gods as subjects,
rather than the early
Christians. When the
sculptor Eberhard re-
torted that the 12
Apostles made such
a wonderful subject,
S c h o p e n h a u e r
replied that he
could take his 12
Philistines and push off to Jerusalem with them. The outraged Nazarenes
nearly beat him up. After that, Schopenhauer avoided
the Greco. (Hermann Kesten, *Poets in the Cafe*)

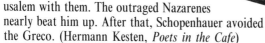

The **Piazza di Spagna**: once a year, on a hot July evening, the
scalinata is transformed into the catwalk of the Roman Alta Moda.
A dream of beautiful clothes and women who get an approving
wink from the shades of Bernini and his companions. After all,
that was the very reason they built the **Barcaccia** fountain (the
barque, by Pietro Bernini the Elder), and façade of the **Propaganda
Fide** (on the right, the exterior by Gian Lorenzo Bernini) and the
steps swinging from concave to convex (Francesco De Sanctis),
with a landing every 12 steps—as an appropriate setting for a
societa spettacolo. But on normal days, too, the piazza 'functions'
as a kind of theatre in which everyone is both audience and actor.
Not always with the full approval of the neighbours, since the
steps are not only the scene of singing and dancing, but also the
meeting-place of Rome's suburbs, where modern architecture can
offer no equivalent.

To the right is Piazza Mignanelli with the **Column of Mary**
(1856), and on the left is the **Accademia Valentino**, an exhibition
centre where the couturier aims to highlight fashion as a cultural
and social phenomenon. In the courtyard (you can go right up to
the porter's lodge) is a massive fragment of an antique bronze
head, a **fountain sculpture** by the Romanian Mitoraj. It's a symbol
of Italy's fashion system, which creates new designs without ever
losing sight of tradition and people. The rags-and-tatters look, the
Count Dracula image or funky dread style have never even managed
a toe-hold in Rome.

Fashion is 'Italy's petroleum'; it underlines the personality, is

easy to wear, avoids extravagance, which sometimes earns it the re-proof of being boring from the Anglo-Saxons. But Italy's couturiers are also manufacturers, and as industrial managers they know better than to unsettle their customers with inconsistencies of style.

The headquarters of the fashion world is below the Piazza di Spagna, between Via Frattina, Via della Croche and the Corso. ROBERTO CAPUCCI only produces one-off models and has no shop as such, only a studio in the Via Gregoriana. His imaginative creations, which he describes as 'fabric sculptures', have ended up in all the great museums of the world as works of art. VALENTINO (men's wear: Via Condotti/corner Mario de Fiori; women's wear: Via Bocca di Leone 15) the classic *haute couture*, with a weakness for flowers and baroque bows (he worships Bernini). He is especially attentive to his many American customers. LAURA BIAGIOTTI (Via Borgognona 43): the 'queen of cashmere' is a fan of soft, warm fabrics. Her sunny nature—and Rome's, too—radiates from the sunny colours of her emphatically feminine creations. FENDI (Via Borgognona 39): the way these famous sisters work furs to Karl Lagerfeld's design is unbeaten anywhere in the world. Magnificent cases, bags, baggy dresses, shoes.

Via Borgogna
5a: FRATELLI ROSETTI—the mystique of Italian shoes.
29: GIANNI VERSACE—men's wear. The creative high-flyer of Italian couture, a blaze of colour from a man from the deep south.

42b: GIANFRANCO FERRE—a trained architect who really constructs his models. Successor to Chanel in France.

Via Condotti
8 and **77:** GUCCI—*Pret-à-porter*, shoes and above all the famous bags and accessories.
20: PIATELLI—a master of tailoring—elegant dresses and suits.
19: BELTRAMI—hand-made shoes, leather goods, one of Rome's most beautiful shops.
72: SALVATORE FERRAGAMO—pioneer of the Italian shoe industry from Florence. Tradition *oblige*.

Piazza di Spagna
27: GENNY—high-class line of Donatella Girombelli (Ancona). Career women love it—practical, durable and elegant.
BYBLOS (Borgognona 7d) transplanted British designers from the same stable, high in the charts with young people.
77b: KRIZIA—primeval (you can see it on their pullovers) and creative enjoyment from Milan's *pret-à-porter*.
78: MISSONI UOMO—Milan's knitwear king with restrained autumnal shades.

Via del Babuino
96A: MISSONI DONNA
102: GIORGIO ARMANI—maestro of the simple, perfectly cut line, jacket virtuoso.

Via del Corso
Casual wear, jeans, shoes between Piazza Parlamento and Piazza del Popolo. Since the street has become a pedestrian zone from Via Tomacelli, the Struscio is back in fashion, that leisurely stroll young people take between 5pm and dinner. Sales, with good bargains: January–February and June–July.

5. Shopping with Luther and Augustus

Window-shopping in the Old City; antiques, crafts and design. Between Piazza del Popolo and Navona. Morning.

Underground A and Rapid Transit Roma Nord 'Flaminio'; bus 2, 90, 95, 115, 119, 202, 204, 490, 495; tram 225. Taxi: Piazza del popolo.

Start off today in **Canova**, Federico Fellini's favourite café. But before we go over to Via Margutta, a short diversion into S **Maria del Popolo**. Renaissance style with a pretty *Birth of Christ* by Pinturicchio (first altar on the right), two dramatic scenes by Caravaggio (on the left next to the high altar), the *Crucifixion of Peter* and the *Conversion of Saul*. The **Cappella Chigi** (second on the left) was designed by Raphael; over the altar is Del Piombo's *Birth of Maria*, on the left Lorenzetti's *Jonah and the Whale*, from a sketch of Raphael, and two sculptures by Bernini, *Habakkuk and the Angel*, who is dragging him by the hair over to *Daniel in the Lion's Den*.

The **S Rita Chapel** (second on the right from the high altar) hides a few juicy stories; the tomb of Vanozza Catanei, mother of three of Cardinal Borgia's four children (he later became Pope Alexander VI); his son Johannes, presumed murdered by his brother Cesare in 1497, is also buried here. Luther lived in the adjacent Augustinian monastery during his four-week stay in Rome in December 1510, and held mass in S Maria del Popolo. Where? The Augustinian patres point as an answer into the **Sacristy**, to Andrea Bregno's altar tabernacle watched over by angels with a Sienese **Madonna** of the early 15th century. A masterpiece created on the order of that same Alexander VI whom Luther hated so much. As an act of 'revenge' for the Reformation, however, the

66

altar was removed from the church, and Bernini himself supervised its departure. In addition, it was said that Luther's cell was turned into a toilet. The monks know nothing about that rumour, because when Valadier the architect transformed the Piazza del Popolo into a parade-ground for divinities, the old monastery was destroyed and all traces of picks and shovels with it.

Past Canova into Via del Babuino, the first left, then right again; **Via Margutta**, once the Montmartre of Rome. But the high prices drove the artists out long ago. Once upon a time, the palazzi of the old city housed a picturesque mixture of rich and poor. Free market economy sorts out the haves from the have-nots; nowadays the best place to live is in the centre, and if you can't afford it, you have to pack your bag. The ones who can afford it are galleries and antique shops. From the ancients (**Silenus**, No 91) via Tyrolean peasant furniture (No 58) to Empire design and art nouveau—**Margutta** has the lot. **De Simone** (No 47) manufactures ceramic items in the strong colours of Sicily. The **Osteria Margutta** is a café for those of aesthetic sensibilities, and serves hearty Roman food. At the end, at Via Alibert 16a, are the **Alinaris**, photographers with the largest collection of 19th century Italian photographs in Italy. Gran and Grandad are alive and well—feel your heart melt a little.

Up the **Via del Babuino** once more (antiques, fashion, avant-garde furniture and lamps), and here let me give you a piece of advice—don't just stare in the windows, go into the shops, ask questions! You don't need to take that heavy ancient Roman Hercules home with you if you don't want to—but when imagination is let loose, when individual taste starts to develop and you begin to find things out, then shopping becomes so much more than just paying for things. And next, a suggestion: wander around for an hour or so in the side-streets between Via del Babuino, del Corso and di Ripetta, and pursue your own interests. Here are some tips. We'll meet again at the bottom end of Via di Ripetta, at Emperor Augustus' mausoleum and altar of peace.

ORAZIO GENNAIO, Via Frattina 41. Masks, carved from wood, terracotta or leather.

LE CRAVATTERIE NAZIONALI, Via Vittoria 62. Ties, ties, ties.

IL DISCOUNT DELL' ALTA MODA, Via Gesù e Maria 16a. Fashion—big names at reasonable prices.

DE CARLIS, Via Vittoria 11. High-class furs.

IL SOLE E LA LUNA, Via dei Greci 12. Jewellery, from wild to classic.

L'Angolo, Via del Corso 510. Missoni's furnishing fabrics.

Leoni Cuoio, Via del Vantaggio 21. Bags and shoes—hand-made and indestructible.

Buccone, Old vault, Via di Ripetta 19. Excellent wines and delicacies.

Restauri Squatriti, Via di Ripetta 29. Dolls and ceramics—in the picturesque restorers' lumber-room.

And back to the ancients—here we are at last in **Via di Ripetta** to see Augustus. His **grave mound**, overgrown with cypresses and unfortunately still closed, housed the biggest concert hall in Rome until 1936. The urns of his wife Livia, his son-in-law Agrippa, stepson Drusus, grandson Germanicus and those of the Caesars Tiberius, Claudius and Nerva were all deposited here. Death and transfiguration are reversed here, because on the other side of the road you can see most of the clan the way they were in life—on the reliefs of the Ara Pacis (open October–March, Tuesday–Saturday 9am–1.30pm, Sunday 9am–1pm, closed Monday; April–September, Tuesday and Saturday also 4–7pm). The **Altar of Augustan Peace** was begun in the year 13BC, when the emperor had knocked the stuffing out of his enemies, both mortal and mental.

A strange construction, always praised but never liked. The interior of the chancel is an object lesson in pagan sacrificial procedure; four steps lead to the ara, and a further four to the altar itself.

Ara Pacis

The priest stood in the centre of the sacred area and could be seen from before and behind. The whole has an atmosphere of solemnity and exaltation. It's a pity that modern architects couldn't think of a better design for the protective enclosure than the clinically cold glass and concrete pavilion.

The exterior walls show Augustus' version of the ideology of divine emperorship. Aeneas, the father of Augustus' house, is seen making a sacrifice to the Penates (to the left of the entrance). On the right is Mars with his sons Romulus and Remus, also part of the lineage. At the back is the Earth Goddess Tellus, with the symbols of Water and Air to represent the Augustan idyll. And of course the goddess Roma is there, albeit as a mere fragment (right). The swan, the sacred bird of Augustus' father Apollo, is seen flying out of thickets of acanthus, ivy, laurel and vines in the lower band of reliefs. All in all, this was an emperor who rose above the world of mere mortals.

The procession, in which he marches behind the lectors with their bundles of twigs with covered head and the gesture of a sacrificial victim, was also intended to edify the Romans. A flashback to Gens Julia, the Kennedys of their time as consuls behind Augustus Tiberius, later Emperor, and Varus, that unfortunate soul in the Teutoburger Forest. Behind the sacrificer with the axe on his shoulder is Agrippa, his adopted son, with his own son Gaius hanging onto his father's tunic, and his wife Julia (daughter of Augustus), Antonia, leading Germanicus as a small boy by the hand (he would later avenge Varus), and her husband Drusus.

Respectability as an idyll, official art; neither Roman nor Greek, neither fish, flesh, fowl nor good red herring. The figures don't come to life, they seem soulless. This is no socialist realism—they were too well educated for that—but the epithet of 'bureaucratic classicism' coined by an art historian is right on target.

In case you want to eat in the area, **Dal Bolognese** (Piazza del Popolo 1) supplies the baroque cuisine of Emilia's capital (70,000 lire). **Porto Di Ripetta** (Via di Ripetta 250) is one of the best fish restaurants in the city (100,000 lire).

6. The Craft of Gold

From mosaics to classy windows, from pocket sundials to 'Ancient Roman' jewellery; the golden lining to crafts in Rome. Afternoon tour.

Bus 52, 53, 56, 81, 85, 90, 95, 119, 492; taxi 'Piazza del Parlamento'.

The bus drops you off in the **Piazza S Silvestro** (main post office); from there, cross the Corso and Piazza del Parlamento; at the back on the right is **Sandro Lebran**, watchmaker and antiques dealer. There you'll find romantic oil paintings of church-tower clocks that really tick, clocks with water-works to make the hands go round, or a chronometer with a cacophony of clucking chickens to mark the hour. Not only do Romans have great respect for the past, they're also magnificent craftsmen.

Both characteristics are united in the antique shops we'll encounter on this expedition through the old city. Of course no walk is complete without a pinch of C&C—culture and churches—but first of all, let's pause for thought in **La Meridiana** (Via Campo Marzio), a bar which takes its name from Emperor Augustus' sundial. German archaeologists unearthed a piece of the sundial in the cellar underneath the bar; you can get the key from the German Archaeological Institute, Via Sardegna 79, Tel: 4817812). The bar serves crisp croissants for breakfast, a large selection of salads at lunchtime and home-made cakes in the afternoon. *Artigiano* is craft, *arte* is art, and the latter was founded on the former. This was the way all Renaissance artists up to Raphael saw it; the master had a business *(bottega)* with assistants and trainees, who sprang in to fill the breach in an emergency, while the boss added the finishing touches if necessary .

Michelangelo painted two heads for Ghirlandaio in this capacity, in the frescos of S Maria Novella in Florence. Craft is a kind of self-realisation, and is enjoying renewed popularity in Italy at the moment. Young people trying to escape from the mundanity of anonymous factory or office jobs have rediscovered the dexterity (*manualità*) of their fathers. And even the greatest Italian artists have never succumbed to the romantic attitude of a genius kissed by the Muse; they remain practical and approachable, seeing themselves as the craftsmen par excellence. Fellini, Abbado and Eco will all discuss the latest football match with you. The Italians' feeling for style and sophistication rakes in the shekels; even the great fashion establishments of France have their fabrics manufactured in Italy, which effectively demolished Lyons' monopoly of the textile market within only a few years after the war. Now Italy is firmly established as the home of quality fabrics.

Down the Via Campo Marzio and across Piazza S Lorenzo in Lucina (on the right is the basilica, with the gridiron on which the saint was tortured). **Il Leoncino** (Via del Leoncino 25) is a treasure-trove of antiques which would beat any English country house into a cocked hat. It was Schiller who said that thoughts were free, and so is looking—the luxury of the average earner. There's a sarcophagus from 575BC, 'for the poor son of one of the Pharaoh's secretaries', according to the owner Signor Antonio. Italians always call the dead *poveri*, even if they were rich. You can buy this macabre specimen for a mere £34,000 (around $68,000).

Claudio Gasparrini (Via Fontanella Borghese), the most important art dealer in Rome, lives in the **Palazzo Ruspoli** with his high-powered collection, which is constantly in a state of flux because of trade, and which he puts on exhibition now and again. Even his office on the street glitters with *grandezza*. Number 10 houses the modern art gallery **Fontanella Borghese**, whose 'stable' includes artists like Pietro Dorazio, and which also has a **Centro Culturale** at No 9, Via della Lupa, with interesting exhibitions. Next door (No 10) is **Carlo Virgilio**, who specialises in the delicate, classic visions of the 19th century (sketches, graphic art)—art which flourished on the dunghill of Ancient Rome, so to speak. No 17 is Rome's first **Grapperia**, with 400 varieties. And if you retrace a couple of steps, you'll find **Vicolo della Torretta 3**, with olive oil, honey, *paté aux truffes* etc, all from the Umbrian estate of Conti Possenti Castelli.

Back to the little market on **Piazza Borghese**, with old books, sketches and engravings. Take a look into the courtyard of the **Palazzo Borghese**, designed in 1560 by Vognola. The three colossal honorary virgins are Giulia Domna (the wife of Septimus Severus), Sabina (Hadrian's wife), and the goddess Ceres. You can see the grounds if you walk around the *cembalo* (harpsichord—the

The heir of Michelangelo

Palazzo's nickname, because of its shape) to Lungotevere. The gallery's art treasures are now in the Museum of the Villa Borghese and the palazzo has been taken over to sell carpets and antiques, enabling you to visit the rooms once inhabited by Napoleon's sister Paolina Borghese. You can see the chapel in the corridor behind the glass door, plus the Cabinet of Mirrors and the rooms painted by Francesco Grimaldi. And if you have a look out of the window at the back on the left, you'll find you're over the Nymphaeum!

Back to the Piazza Fontanella Borghese—in the Vicolo del Divino Amore, No 18a, **Marco Zanin** produces his jewellery creations with a tendency towards deco. Go on to the right to Piazza Firenze (old engravings), Via d'Ascanio (rustic furniture, Calabresian folk-art, vases, carpets etc), Via dei Portoghesi (National Church) to the Via dell'Orso, Via Pianellari, Via dei Gigli d'Oro, Vicolo della Palomba—art, crafts, antiques. And here are some tips for this maze of alleyways: **Massimo Maria Melis** (Orso 57) has adopted the timeless forms of antiquity in his gold work (you can watch him at work). Silvana Fiore's **Marmo** (No 63) will make old mosaics, marble columns and so on to your specifications, and isn't even wildly expensive (the workshop, where half-a-dozen men are beavering away, is particularly interesting). And if you're really keen to take a little bit of Rome or Etruria home with you, try **Gea Arte Antica** (No 82), where you can find tiny vases for as little as 200,000 lire. And don't worry, Tullio Diamanti is a respectable dealer who works with the Directorship of Antiquities. He also has Bucchero vases for around £10,000 ($20,000) in stock, but you can buy a decent jug—including the necessary expertise—for around £700 ($1,400).

At the bottom of Orso is the **Osteria dell' Orso**, where Goethe spent his time in Rome. Empire fans should go up the steps to feast their eyes in the **Museo Napoleonico**; after all, the Empire's second capital was full of his relations (Via Zardanelli 1; open 9am–2pm, Sunday 9am–1pm, Tuesday and Thursday also 5–8pm, closed Monday). And take the time to look into S Agostino and see Jacopo Sansovino's *Madonna del Parto* (of the Birth). It's a prime showpiece of Renaissance art—this is no representative of compulsory motherhood with an air of suffering and endurance, such as you find in northern regions, but a real live goddess! The Prophet Isaiah (third pillar on the left) is by Raphael, with Michelangelo obviously looking over his shoulder. The Byzantine Madonna on the high altar is said to have been painted by Luke the Apostle himself—faith doesn't just move mountains, it also juggles with dates. But the main attraction here is the *Madonna dei Pellegrini*. Why did Caravaggio and his dynamic chiaroscuro create such uproar among the cultured citizens of 1605? Maria is a fine figure of a woman, the boy Jesus has a little satchel and the pair of pilgrims haven't washed their feet for days; altogether too realistic for academics, who believed that the purpose of art was to edify and idealise.

This corner has three restaurants which can be recommended: **Il Convivio** (Via dell'Orso 44, 70,000 lire): lobster salad, fillet of turbot with courgettes and white truffle. **L'Orso 80** (No 33, 40,000 lire) offers a wide selection of appetisers, *spaghetti alla matriciana*, grilled meat, or excellent pizza—in which case you can get away with only 25,000 lire. **La Majella** (Piazza S Apollinare 4, 50,000 lire) has fresh sea-fish and Abruzzo lamb—you can eat in the open air in summer.

Shopping Tips

Coloured windows—art nouveau etc—made to measure by Isabella Spani and Gianni Jacovazzi at **Trasparenza**, Via di S Eustachio 12 (by the Pantheon). **Magicians' props** by the ton at **Franco Contigliozzi**, Via in Aquiro 70 (Piazza Montecitorio)—including the box for sawing your wife in half . **Fireplaces**, antique or new, plus hearth sets and other associated items: **Il Camineto**, Via del Leone 23 (Piazza Borghese) **Sundials**: You can fulfil this particular fantasy at **Adrian Rodriguez**, Via del Moro 59 (Trastevere). All of them are handmade, and some are small enough to take away with you. All the **monastery liqueurs** in Italy and other monastery products—wine, honey, chocolate, sweets, biscuits, herbs, soaps, bath oils, perfumes and cosmetic oils at **Ai Monasteri**, Piazza delle Cinque Lune 76. **Stuffed animals**, hunting trophies, butterflies, shells, fossils and minerals at **Fratelli Bertoni**, Via S Agostino 5 (Piazza Navona). **Curiosities for cats** at Monique Gregory's off-beat **Chat Amour**, Piazza Rondanini 48. **Wicker furniture** and everything you can think of made from bamboo, willow and straw—also made to your specifications—at **Vincenzo Caiani** and his colleagues in Via del Teatro Valle 31 and in Via Sediari (the chair-makers) behind Navona.

7. The Basilica of the Clean Sweepers

'Here I am a man, here I can be a man', said the ancient Romans when they went to the baths, the meeting-place for everyone from the Emperor downwards. From the Caracalla Baths to the Via Appia and the Catacombs. Morning tour.

Underground 'Circo Massimo'; buses 90, 93, 118, 613, 671; taxi 'Terme di Caracalla'.

'Soul of Man, thou art like water', spake Goethe; by those lights, Rome was exceedingly soulful. Eleven large aqueducts and 247 cisterns kept 212 fountains flowing and provided million of gallons of water every day to quench the city's thirst.

The hot baths were the temples of the water cult. When you see their reconstructions, you feel almost sorry that you weren't there in person to experience the celebration of cleanliness and fitness. But don't let yourself be deceived by the 'morning after the night before' atmosphere of the **Caracalla Baths**, opened in 216. The extensive complex of ruins, occupying $334m^2$ (3,600 square feet), was once as ornate as a Victorian railway station—with, of course, a different purpose (open Sunday, Monday 9am–1pm, other days from 9am to one hour before sunset).

We enter the realm of the squeaky-clean through the workout room. Next door is the gymnasium with mosaic floors; through the cloakroom (*vestibolo*) is the Tepidarium (lukewarm), on the left the Frigidarium (cold), on the right the Caldarium, where Pavarotti bellows out *Celeste Aida* in the summer festival—the sauna, for sweating and losing weight. For the rest, there's a Latin and Greek library, a Mithraeum as a chapel, conference and lecture rooms—not to mention all the massage rooms and the open-air stadium. The rich also had a comfortable bathroom at home.

But the public baths offered much more than bathing, namely the chance to meet people divested of formalities. Pliny the Elder told of his nephew, who dictated letters to his secretary while in the pool, and of women who defied all the interdicts and codes of honour in favour of naturist practises—and worse—with the men. Martial wrote amused epigrams on the subject. Hadrian segregated the sexes into separate rooms. One day the emperor saw an old man rubbing his back against a marble column because he didn't have enough money for

The Tombs of the Scipioni

a masseur; the man was immediately presented with the requisite slave, as a gift. Baths were part of the legionaries' travelling requisites; wherever you found a Roman dug-out, you'd find the Romans bathing. Tell me how you wash, and I'll tell you who you are: washing was by no means a private affair. Seneca gives a detailed report on Cornelius Scipio, known as Africanus because of his victory over Hannibal; this gentleman had a dark, narrow bathroom in which he would wash his arms and legs every day, and the whole of his body every nine days. Augustus avoided water in winter, but during the imperial era several dips a day were considered good form. Tacitus warned that 'baths, wine and women are corrupting our bodies'.

On to the **Tombs of the Scipioni** in the Via di Porta S Sebastiano, 10 minutes' walk away, or two stops on the 118 bus (open 9am–1.30pm, Sunday 9am–1pm, closed Monday; in summer also open 4–7pm on Tuesday, Thursday and Saturday). Here are the sarcophagi of the family which supplied Rome's best generals in the third and second centuries BC. A three-storey house dating from the third century, a columbarium (dovecote), as the tombs with niches for the urns were known. You need a guide and a key to get to the better-kept Columbarium of the freedman Pomponius Hylas and his wife Vitalinis, with its plasterwork and frescoes from the first century.

And after the Arch of Drusus, the **Porta di S Sebastiano**, with the **Museo delle Mura Romane** (open 9am–1.30pm, Tuesday also 4–7pm, closed Monday). What have the northerners of today got in common with the East Goths? Nothing really. And yet there is some kind of connection with Theodoric, known to German heroic

Cecilia in the Catacombs of Calixtus

sagas as Dietrich of Bern (ie Verona). In 536 his successor Witichis sent Germanic warriors running against the brick bulwark—all 18km (11 miles) of it, 8m (25ft) high and 4m (13ft) thick—but in vain; the death toll was high, and contributed considerably towards the decline of this people only a few years later. Today the sounds of battle have stilled and birdsong has replaced them, for the wall blocks off the noise of the city and cuts through fields and vegetable gardens. Romans once again have their ancestors to thank for this green belt; no building is permitted on its ruins.

On the **Via Appia Antica**, the 'queen of roads' lined with tombs and dating from the year 312BC, you're liable to be run off the road by the traffic; the road has no pavement. A better idea is to take the 118 bus to the wall gate after S Callisto (ask the driver) or continue straight on to S Sebastiano. And one of the most interesting legends is set at the little church of Domine—Quo Vadis, on the left; Peter, fleeing Rome and the persecution of the Christians, sees Jesus coming towards him on the Via Appia. 'Master, where are you going?' The answer: 'To Rome, to be crucified a second time.' Which effectively sealed the fate of the chief apostle.

In Quo Vadis there is a footprint said to be that of Christ, but which is in fact a votive offering made by a pagan after a safely completed journey. Religion is layered upon religion; this is also apparent in the **Catacombs**, which, by the way, were never used by the Christians as a hiding-place: the stink of decay in the air would have precluded that.

In the three pagan **tombs of S Sebastiano**, some of the finest art to be found in the catacombs, the Christians simply imposed their individual note on the pictures and plasterwork already in existence; it wasn't far from Apollo to the Good Shepherd. And as the pagan frescoes are the same quality as the Christian ones, art historians tend towards the belief that painters and masons were non-denominational; he who paid the piper called the tune.

Goethe on S Sebastiano: 'On my first steps in these musty chambers, I was filled with such a profound unease that I immediately returned to daylight.' He sensed something sinister, for there are certain stories which have never died out. Even today, guides in S Callisto tell of pagan parents who let their children starve to death, and who would also have let their offspring rot in the gutter if the Christians had not collected the corpses and given them a decent burial in the catacombs.

We've already vented our opinion about the Romans' faultless sense of hygiene—it wasn't until the years of Christianity that plague began to stalk Europe. The catacombs are looked after by religious orders and are primarily of religious rather than academic significance. Recent research brought to light that the early Christians were generally poor, married very young and died before reaching any advanced age. They were frequently unable to write and marked their graves with coins, shells, fragments of glass or pottery or, as in one case, with a small figure carved in limestone. Their tombstones were not as sophisticated as those of the heathens, and their lack of education could be clearly seen in their uncertain script full of mistakes in spelling and grammar.

After this intermezzo in the underworld labyrinth—170,000 are said to be buried in **S Callisto**—we'll return to daylight and the Appian Way. You can avoid the traffic between S Callisto and S Sebastiano by cutting across the grounds of the monastery. If you want to continue through the graveyard past the **Round Tower of Cecilia Metella**, you can get a brochure describing more or less every stone of the Appian Way from the **Ente Provinciale per il Turismo di Roma** (Via Parigi 5, Stazioni Termini, also available from CIT, Piazza della Repubblica 68).

The Aurelian Walls

Excellent food and the chance to eat it in the open air in fine weather, can be enjoyed at **Cecilia Metella** (Via Appia Antica 125, 40,000 lire); the excellent menu has a touch of international influence. For somewhere more traditionally Roman, with the bonus of a cosy open fire in wintry weather, **Antica Archeologia** (Via Appia Antica 139, 25,000 lire) is worth visiting.

8. The Tosca Tour

Nietzsche said that all love seeks destruction. From S Andrea della Valle via the Palazzo Farnese to Castel Sant' Angelo in the footsteps of Puccini's Tosca. On the way Campo de' Fiori, the most important market in the old town. Morning tour.

Bus 26, 62, 64, 70, 81, 186, 492; taxi 'Sant' Andrea della Valle'.

Opera is on a different plane. *Vissi d'Arte*, sings Tosca; 'Only to beauty does my life belong'. A shiver runs up your spine with the sheer excitement of all that *bel canto* lust and passion. Of course it's only fiction; but remember what Raphael thought, that art must be truer than truth, more real than reality? And the melodrama is the fulfilment of this ideal transformed into music.

Act One: The church of **S Andrea della Valle**, first side chapel on the right. The **Cappella Lancelotti** is the perfect setting for listening to Puccini over a Walkman (not too loud)—it's crammed with operatic pathos. Carlo Fontana pulled out all the stops in 1670: marble, even some straight from Africa, black, white, *verde antico*, alabaster, jasper from Sicily, swathes of gold and sheets of emerald. A relief of Joseph being sent to Egypt by the angel. Angels rejoicing, and of course the commissioners of all this glory, large as life (nearly) and twice as natural, kneeling in cardinals' garb on their coffins. How will they react to Tosca? Magnanimously, or anxiously, because the wave of sex and crime rolling towards them is threatening to disturb the heavenly peace?

The monster and sexpot in the whole affair is none other than Scarpia, the Papal Chief of Police. It should be added that *Tosca* was premiered in Rome in 1900; we'll come across quite a lot of the anti-clericalism of those times. Angelotti, consul of the Roman Republic, has broken out of Castel Sant' Angelo and seeks refuge in the chapel. He is helped by Cavardossi the painter. Tosca is torn with jealousy. At this stage, have a look at the dome; the spandrels

At the Campo de' Fiori

house Domenichino's *Four Evangelists*, which threw Goethe into such raptures, while the shell displays the *Glory of Paradise* by Giovanni Lanfranco—the church's chief treasure, together with Domenichino's pictures of St Andrew in the apse. But the enormous *Crucifixion of the Apostle* (in the body of the apse, by Mattia Preti), an eyesore of titanic proportions, looks like a parody of Michelangelo.

Turn right out of the church, past the ruins of the Pompeius Theatre, cross the Piazza del Paradiso and you arrive at **Campo de' Fiori**, the old city's chief market. Fruit, vegetables, fish, sheeps' milk cheeses, lamb and kid meat. Number 43 houses the Viola Brothers' **Norcineria**, highly praised and paradise for anyone who wants to make a pig of him/herself—so to speak. Sausages (*salsicce, luganighe, ciauscolo*) and hams from Norcia in Umbria, which, incidentally, was the birthplace of St Benedict. **Minetto**, in Via del Giubbonari 54, is a typical Old Roman café where your *cappuccino* arrives with a pile of whipped cream or a blob of fresh curd cheese. Let's stop a minute at the 'black man' of bronze, gazing phlegmatically at the Campo de' Fiori with a book in his hand and pigeons on his habit. The monument dates from 1887 and is dedicated to Giordano 'Bruno, from the century he anticipated. Here, where the fire of the stake burned'; on 17 February 1600.

Another hammer of anti-papal feelings. Bruno died a heretic's death in the flames of the Counter-Reformation because he constructed a metaphysical edifice upon the discoveries Copernicus had made in the emptiness of space. The earth's orbit around the sun was only the basis. Bruno announced from on high that the universe was a system composed of countless worlds; every world revolved around its sun, developed and died, given life by the 'pulse of the One divine All-Life', of which Man is a reflection and an element, since without God there can be no existence. This monk was a mystic, a poet and—a shallow summing-up—an optimist. In his opinion God was an artist, constantly creating harmony. This inspired man ignored the abysses believed to lodge within Creation and recognised its beauty as a whole.

Why did Bruno fan the fires of the Inquisition with his theories, like Galileo, more harmless, four decades later? Our planet a speck of dust in space? This contradicted the Bible, the Book of Books, which teaches that Man is the pinnacle of creation whose centre is the earth. This placed Christ's martyrdom on the Cross and his work of salvation and redemption in a completely different light when related to the scale of Bruno's ideas. And more concrete considerations also worked against Bruno. His image of Man was

The 'Old Quarter'

based more on Renaissance characteristics than on the theory of original sin, and could manage perfectly well without the revelation and the sacrament of penance. Science and philosophy which conducted research or devised new directions of thought without taking the official Church into account, further limited its role. Galileo was forgiven by the Vatican because natural science is like two and two, always four. There's no arguing with the fact that the earth goes round the sun. Bruno's crimes, on the other hand, attacked fundamental beliefs, and even nowadays there are people who would like to sweep him, and his challenging ideas, under the carpet of history.

The Via de Balestrari leads you to the **Piazza Capo di Ferro**, with corner shops, craftsmen in smoky vaults, old, simple *baretti*. Here, around the Campo de' Fiori, flourishes the Rome of yesteryear. If you walk through the quarter after dark and look into the lit windows of the upper stories, you'll see painted and panelled ceilings en masse.

The **Palazzo Spada**, with its parade of Roman heroes on the façade, is rather overgrown for the little piazza at its feet. Romulus and Trajan, a huge plinth and an airy arrangement of garlands, medallions, nudes—you can see exactly what happened to the Renaissance up to 1560. It's funny that this mannerist conglomeration was commissioned from Giulio Mazzoni by cardinals, of all people. A carabiniere stands guard at the gate, because this is the seat of the Italian Parliament, but go ahead and look at the courtyard, where the mythical heroics are continued. Look to the right into Gianni the porter's lodge, by Parin del Vaga, who we'll meet again later in Castel Sant' Angelo; his *Rape of Helena* here makes this probably the loveliest porter's lodge in all Rome.

On the left of the courtyard, through a glass door, you can see *la prospettiva*, appearance masquerading as reality—Borromini's

80

Colonnada is a mere 8m (27ft) long, but the columns decrease sharply in size towards the back; stupendously effective. The garden is a 'Roman dream', with orange trees, magnolias, palms, cats and, alas, a lot of parked cars. On the left is the entrance to the **Galleria Spada** (9am–2pm, Sunday 9am–1pm), the private collection of Cardinal Bernardino Spada; the ruling classes in the Rome of the 17th century lived amidst an abundance of paintings. Those of Titian, Andrea del Sarto, Rubens, Reni and Guercino are outstanding. On the left of the exit, in the vault of Vicolo de Venti 5 at **Guiseppina Princi**, you can get made-to-order inlaid work in stone *(pietra dura)*, columns old and new and tiles in original designs. And **Piazza Farnese 52** displays the finest Italy has to offer in floor and wall coverings (wallpaper, tiles and so on).

Act Two: Palazzo Farnese. The galleria painted by Annibale Caracci can only be visited on Sundays from 10am–noon, since it houses the French Embassy. This is where Scarpia the monster has Cavaradossi tortured and where he is stabbed by Tosca, whose love he tried to extort. Take a look through the windows at the magnificent ceiling. The layout and façade make it a pure Renaissance palazzo with a harmony 'attained where nothing can be altered, nothing added or taken away without diminishing the perfection of the whole' (G L Alberti). The two fountain basins on the piazza are of Egyptian granite and they originally formed part of the washing facilities in the Caracalla Baths.

The Via del Mascherone takes you to the **Via Giulia** with its art galleries and antique shops, laid out as a showpiece thoroughfare by Pope Julius II. The first important stop is the **Pinacotheca** on the left, with Italian paintings of the 19th century. Number 193 houses the **Antiquariato Valligiano** with elegant furniture. Then go back, under the bridge which the Farneses built to connect their gardens.

Look into the **Galleria Arco Farnese** (No 180), and into the churches along the road until you come to **S Giovanni dei Fiorentini**, with its 'brute beast' of a priest, Don Mario Canciani. Monsignore is a great animal lover and blesses dogs, cats, parrots and canaries in his Mass. 'Animals have their Paradise, too—we see them again in the hereafter', maintains the priest, who tries to persuade the Italians to drop one particular religious custom—eating lamb at Easter. When the Pope was made a present of just such a lamb, he declared, 'We had better ask Monsignore Canciani what to do with it.' It now grazes in the Papal gardens. Bernini's baroque style is embodied by the **Ponte S Angelo** and its ten angels bearing the instruments of Christ's suffering.

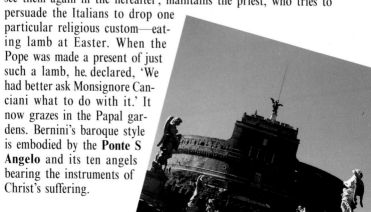

Castel Sant' Angelo

Act Three: Castel Sant' Angelo (open 9am–2pm, Sunday 9am–1pm, Monday 2–6pm). Cavaradossi sings, 'And the stars shine', and is promptly shot. Tosca hurls herself to her death. The bigger the tomb, the less likely its occupant is to rest in peace eternally. The model for Hadrian's top-hat, 64m (209ft) in diameter, was one of the Seven Wonders of the World, the tomb of Mausolus at Halicarnassos, from which our word 'mausoleum' is derived. The building was originally enclosed in marble, of which some fragments with reliefs remain. Its position, however, had enormous strategic importance, meaning that by the early Middle Ages the block had become the hard-core of Roman and papal defences. In 1527, Clemens VII was besieged by Charles V's troops for seven months before he finally capitulated.

Fountain, flowerpot . . . a coffin is a multi-functional object, as you can see all over Rome. Hadrian's was used first as a tomb for Pope Innocent II and was then dismantled, whereupon parts of it were taken for Otto II in St Peter's. Today the lid is in use as a font in St Peter's. Exalted art can be seen in the Papal Chambers, by Pierin del Vaga, Sicciolante da Sermoneta, Giuliano Romano.

Conversing Angels

Originally a Roman quadriga stood on the building, replaced in 1752 with the bronze *Archangel Michael* by Pietro Verschaffelt. In the meantime, the quadriga has been replaced a little further up the Tiber. Yet another blow struck by the Italian laity against the papacy, this time around the turn of the century.

9. Popes, Il Papa and Palaces

From the magnificence of the 'black aristocrats' to the shadow of the ghetto; the Papal Rome of yore played by its own rules, as this walk through the old city will show.

Bus 44, 46, 56, 81, 85, 90, 95, 116, 492; from the Corso down Via Lata to (taxi:) 'Piazza Collegio Romano'.

'The days when the popes still had families' could be the title of our visit to Innocent X in the Palazzo Doria Pamphili (open Tuesday, Friday, Saturday, Sunday 10am–1pm, tour of the private chambers at 11am and noon). Popes and cardinals may not actually have children, but they have relatives; and Giambattista Pamphili, crowned on 14 September 1644 and hanging today in the Galleria under No 339, was no exception.

'And that canaille bears the name Innocent!' wrote Eckart Peterich scornfully. Velasquez' analysis of the pontifical character portrays him as a man with inner conflicts, a brooder. However, Leopold von Ranke, an expert on popes, decided that the painter's impression was false, and credited Innocent with being 'approachable and good-tempered'. 'Order and peace in Rome were matters of especial concern to him'. Things didn't look so rosy for order and peace among his own family, however. His sister-in-law, Donna Olympia Maidalchina—also in the gallery, as a bust by Alessandro Algardi—adopted the role of a real *prima donna*; 'Newly arrived ambassadors always visited her first. Cardinals displayed her portrait in their chambers, as one would display the portrait of a prince or ruler; foreign courts tried to win her favour by presenting her with gifts' (Ranke).

This family wasn't just a family affair, and when Donna Olympia had a set-to with her daughter-in-law both Spain and France attempted to turn the row to their own advantage. This was nothing unusual in Rome; as soon as a Roman was elected Pope, his family assumed the position of the ruling clan. The Vicars of Christ were usually getting on in years, however, so the glory only lasted until its originator died. There has never been a Papal dynasty, but the great Roman families were more conscious of matters of dynasty than families elsewhere. Having one of your own on the Throne of St Peter was a unique chance to gain social and financial security. Relatives and supporters were elected to cardinals' positions, creating a block

Galleria Doria Pamphili

of power which survived the pope around whom it was built. The term 'nepotism' came from Cardinal Nepote, the Pope's nephew, who played a key role in the Vatican.

The Popes built the Palazzi Borghese, Barberini, Farnese, Chigi, Colonna and Pamphili for their families and stuffed them full of art. Elections were frequently also occasions for settling scores; Innocent X confiscated property from the Barberini, who had been his predecessors in power with Urban VIII. He waged a successful war against the Farnese. The constant changes of personnel on the Throne of St Peter prevented Rome from becoming a normal city with centrally based urban planning; instead, it remained a patchwork quilt of family groups, shifting constantly at each new election.

From Raphael to Rubens, from Caravaggio to Titian, the guide-book available at the ticket office gives helpful information on the artists and subjects of the 450 works on show. A diversion through the private apartments takes you through the conservatory and the *fumoire* into the Sala Andrea Doria, Charles V's admiral. At the Battle of Lepanto (now Naupaktos in Greece) on 7 October 1571, which broke the supremacy of the Turkish fleet, Doria was in charge of the right wing of the Christian forces. A rather irreverent question comes to mind with all of these trophies and tapestries depicting raging battles: are men permitted, when in unusual or extraordinary situations, simply to dance? Gregorovius stated firmly they were not, in his essay *The Ghetto and the Jews in Rome* of 1853. 'Europeans often perceive an element of caricature in the true Jewish manner, which appears as ludicrous as King David's capering, clownish dance before the Ark of the Covenant.' The author of those words wasn't actually anti-Semitic, but he was certainly a Northern European.

Before the 202 Christian galleons moved into the Turks, the Supreme Commander Don Juan of Austria ordered the fleet to form a semicircle around his flagship. An orchestra played on deck, and the Hapsburger with the Spanish blood danced on the bridge of his ship for the sailors, oblivious to the battle and to everything around him. Then the battle against the 282 ships flying the crescent flag was opened. The allied fleet was smaller in number, but superior in fire-power; 1,814 Christian marksmen gained the upper hand against 750 Mohammedans.

The bravest fighters were to be found on the left flank in the 105 Venetian galleons of Agostino Barbarigos, who fell in the battle. At the centre, Don Juan grappled with the Turks, while

84

Doria bombarded them from a distance. His descendants, with at least a capful of Hohenstaufen blood in their veins, brought more and more treasures to their residence; Lippi, Memling, Bronzino, Lotto, Beccafumi, a balancing act of beauty between mannerism and rococo. Don Juan's dance went on, but this time on the tightrope of sophisticated taste.

From the Piazza del Collegio Romano on the left into the Via della Gatta, then bear to the right to the Piazza Grazioli 17a and **Studio Keire**, furniture designers. The 'Pigne' are interesting, pine cones made from reddish vulcanite from Latin America after an ancient design (think of the Cortile della Pigna in the Vatican). Have a look at **Tessilroma**, Via del Plebescito 101b—an old vault full to the ceiling of bales of fabric. Next door is the courtyard of the Palazzo Altieri, Pope Clement X's elegiac visiting card. Opposite is the **Church del Gesù**, of the Jesuits, founded by Ignatius Loyola. It's a typical design with mannerist architecture and a baroque interior, which has been imitated hundreds of times in every Catholic country. The ceiling fresco *Triumph of the Name of Jesus* is a celebration of the Counter-Reformation by the Genoese Baciccio. The radiance of salvation streams out of the frame provided by the architect Vignola, catapulting saints and angels across the surface of the dome; transforming the fresco into sculpture.

By the end of the 18th century, Rome had digested the trauma of Protestant schism. In the Chapel of St Ignatius, Andrea Pozzo, himself a Jesuit, pulls out all the stops of theatricality. Ignatius—once clad in silver until Napoleon, that well-known art thief, came along—shines like Superman taking flight, but the heretics being dragged into the abyss of Hell by the diabolical snake, are vaguely reminiscent of Laocoon of antique times, who also tried to throw a spanner in Heaven's works.

Cross the Piazza del Gesù to the **Area Sacra del Largo Argentina** with the Republican forum, where you'll see the foundations of three temples from the fourth to the first century BC. It's not certain which gods they were dedicated to. In the Capitoline Museum there is a colossal statue of Juno which was found here, with marble 'flesh' and bronze robes. Along the front of the piazza is the **Teatro Argentina**, opened in 1731, in which Rossini's *Barber of Seville* had its premiere in 1816—and flopped. To its left, in the Via Barberi 7, is **Spazio Sette**, a furniture store with lively designs. The upper storey houses the frescoes of the Palazzo Lazzaroni from the 18th century, well

Fontana delle Tartarughe

worth looking at. There are hundreds of ceilings like this one in Rome, and most guide-books don't even deign to mention them.

Cross the Largo Arenuela, down the Via S Elena and the Via Falegnami to Piazza Mattei and Taddeo Landini's 'Tortoise Fountain' of 1584. The fountain is formed by four slender youths, holding onto a dolphin with one hand and trying to push a tortoise (a later addition) into the upper basin with the other. Opposite is the Casa Matei, yet another monument to Roman family closeness; in Renaissance times, the whole of this area was overrun by hundreds of members of the same family. The steps lead up to a loggia on the first floor, and since the Council disco occupies the house, you can go right up to the top storey (great view!).

Piazza Lovatelli and Via S Angelo in Peschia lead to the Portico d'Ottavia, the remains of a hall of columns 118m (388ft) wide and 135m (444ft) deep, erected by Metellus in 147BC as display premises for the works of art seized in Greece, and thus the first Roman museum. Augustus dedicated the complex to his sister Octavia.

'It was here that Vespasian and Titus led the procession of victory over Israel with ceremonial displays', noted Gregorovius.

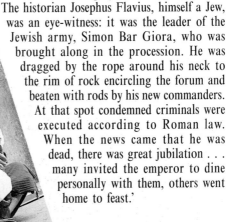

The historian Josephus Flavius, himself a Jew, was an eye-witness: it was the leader of the Jewish army, Simon Bar Giora, who was brought along in the procession. He was dragged by the rope around his neck to the rim of rock encircling the forum and beaten with rods by his new commanders. At that spot condemned criminals were executed according to Roman law. When the news came that he was dead, there was great jubilation . . . many invited the emperor to dine personally with them, others went home to feast.'

After this defeat the Jews scattered across the empire. Many moved to Rome to seek lodgings in Trastevere. Their position was not improved by Christianity's later victory, which branded them 'murderers of God' and heretics. Paul IV Caraffa ordered that on 26 July 1556 they should be forcibly moved to what is now the ghetto, which 'Jew-pit' they would only be permitted to leave if wearing a yellow hat (for men) or a yellow veil (for women), even during daylight hours. Jewish doctors were forbidden to treat Christian patients, and there was a general ban on contact with Christians, on trading and on practising a craft.

On the right is the Victorian synagogue, with an Assyrian and Babylonian-style façade. On the left are wall tableaux from the Teatro Marcello, built by Augustus for 14,000 spectators. Later, aristocratic Roman families settled within the ancient walls, and finally the Orsini built their palazzo here. Straight ahead is the church of S Angelo in Pescheria, where 300 Jews were forced by papal decree to listen to a Christian sermon every Saturday. Gregorovius' view: 'Even on the Sabbath, henchmen of the police force were seen entering the ghetto and driving Jews into the church lashing their whips… A guard at the door counted those entering; within the church guards supervised the attentiveness of those present, and if a Jew seemed listless or sleepy, he was awoken with lashes and blows.'

The ghetto was overflowing, and thus dirty and unhygienic. The Tiber floods were particularly troublesome, since they submerged lower-lying parts of the ghetto. The troops of the French Revolution opened the gates, Pius VII closed them again in 1814, and finally, in 1847, Pius IX had the inhuman walls in the heart of Rome torn down. You can still walk through the ghetto, where nowadays many Roman traders sell china and household goods. **Piperno** (Monte de Cenci 9) has kosher food. **Dolceroma** (Via del Portico d'Ottavia 20b) is full of temptations for the sweet-toothed—Stefano Ceccarelli, the owner, trained in the Hotel Regina in Vienna. **Il Forno del Ghetto** (same street) has Jewish cakes and breads.

If you feel like another dip into antiquity, the church of S Nicola in Carcere (Via del Teatro di Marcello) was once a pagan temple. A couple of steps further on is the Temple of Vesta (5th century BC) and the Forum Boarium.

The Temple of Vesta

10. Ceaser's Comic

Trajan's Column—making your mark, outliving your mortality. From the Imperial forum to Michelangelo's Tomb of Julius and the subterranean basilica of S Clemente.

Bus 44, 48, 57, 64, 65, 70, 85, 87, 186, 710, 718, 719; taxi 'Piazza Venezia'.

The comic strip is made of marble and is over 198m (650ft) long. Not 'Asterix and Caesar's Gift', but 'Trajan and the Dacians' is the name of the band of reliefs at the back of the Piazza Venezia, a chronicle in pictures of the two campaigns which knocked the mighty tribe on the Danube into Roman or Romanic (today Romanian) shape. Naval manoeuvres, animal sacrifices, entrenchments, ambushes, battles, pep-talks to the soldiers and all the other things that happened in the Balkan wars between 101 and 107. The creator of the 2,500 elegantly designed figures is unnamed, but the spiral frieze almost 30.5m (100ft) high, consisting of 18 marble rings around 3.5m (12ft) in diameter, set one above the other with a spiral staircase running up the centre, is one of the major achievements of Roman sculpture; what's more, this 'stone papyrus' has retained its clarity and plasticity and can be easily 'read' from a distance.

Now and again blood flows, but the most remarkable feature is the portrayal of the enemy as courageous, dignified and intelligent. The emperor, in true comic-strip tradition, is represented as omnipresent and charismatic, around 60 times over (or more).

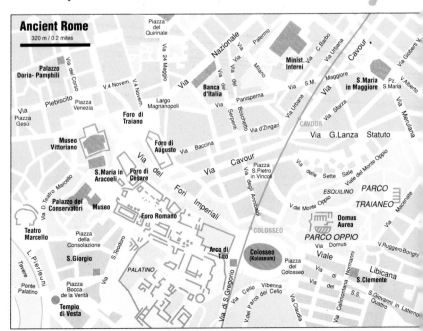

Moreover, his ashes were buried at the foot of the column. Does that make it a monument to vanity, this 'pointing finger' of the Caesar? Well, not only that; the urge to announce 'Here I am, I was here' doesn't only befall little people who scribble names and messages on walls and monuments; even Vicars of Christ fall victim to it. Every new construction, every work of restoration has to be signed. Paul V Borghese, who had temples demolished at the Forum to provide marble for his water system, announces his presence on the front of St Peter's in letters so huge you'd think he'd built it himself. Paul VI Montini (1963–78) also made sure he was immortalised. Only Karel Wojtyla isn't following in their footsteps, but then he is from another world.

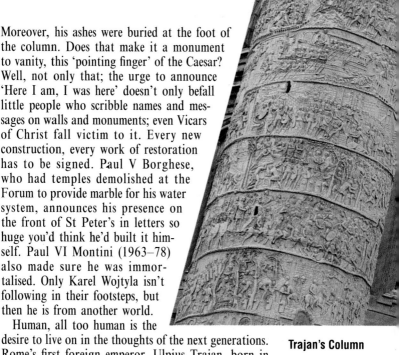

Trajan's Column

Human, all too human is the desire to live on in the thoughts of the next generations. Rome's first foreign emperor, Ulpius Trajan, born in Seville, swamped the city in huge buildings, whose ruins help nowadays in piecing together the fragments of the past. His finest column could be looked into from all sides and from its entire height, flanked as it was by Latin and Greek libraries. The column, topped by a statue of Peter (Tomaso Della Porta, 1587) is 38m (125ft) high including the base. The inscription at its foot recounts that Apollodoros, its builder, reduced the height of the hill on the right by the same amount to build the Trajan Markets. Before we go up the steps to the entrance on the Via IV Novembre 94, here's a little help in orientation for the Imperial Forum—the largest, at 301 x 185m (987 x 608ft).

Under the twin churches of S Maria di Loreto (on the left, foundation stone laid in 1507) and SS Nome di Maria (built after the Turkish Siege of Vienna in 1683), are the foundations of the hall of columns which ran in the form of a semi-circle around the temple of the deified Trajan and his wife Plotina. There were originally 95 columns in front of the main memorial column, supporting the roof of the Basilica Ulpia and its five naves. In front, at precisely the spot where the two paths cross, stood the Emperor's imposing memorial. The East Roman emperor Constantine II contemplated the memorial in 357 and remarked sorrowfully that he would never get such a horse as that. His companion, the Persian Prince Hormisdas, replied, 'But first you would have to build your horse a stable like this.'

Trajan's Markets (open 9am–1.30pm, Sunday 9am–1pm; from 1 April–30 September also Tuesday, Thursday, Saturday 4–7pm; closed Monday) were rebuilt to form a multi-purpose centre with

Welcome refreshment

150 shops, assembly rooms, and the offices of the imperial financial and general administration, which was also responsible for the distribution of free food among the Roman masses. A large find of amphorae and earthenware vases, today displayed in the upper storeys, came from the storehouse. The classical brickwork on the *exedra,* or area of seats, is particularly fine and glows as if lit from within in the evening sun.

Back to Trajan's Column. His forum was divided off from that of Augustus by a triumphal arch which today adjoins the mediaeval 'House of the Knights of Malta'. The steps on the left at the bottom lead to the entrance of the Temple of Mars Ultor, built for Drusus and Germanicus. Further on is the Nerva Forum, with two columns and some relief fragments of the Temple of Minerva, depicting women working under the protection of the goddess—whose presence is still in evidence. Behind the scrap of worn grass with the benches is the Torre dei Conti—a meeting-point for the whole area—and the Via Madonna dei Monti. In No 112, opposite the Hotel Forum, is the beauty salon of Ellen Gross, a native of Munich who, since setting up shop in Rome, has specialised in the cosmetics of the Ancient Romans.

Everyone knows that Poppaea bathed daily in asses' milk and Cleopatra had a farm on the Red Sea dedicated solely to growing the plants needed for her skin care. *Cura dabit faciem*—care creates beauty—wrote Ovid. But high-class men used perfume as well, and the Comitato Nazionale delle Ricerche (CNR), the national scientific research institute, began a project years ago which asked the question 'what did men like Julius Caesar smell like when they were engaged in manoeuvres of the *ars amandi* kind rather than the *bellum gallicum*?' After much consultation of old folios and mixing of essences, the conclusion was drawn that they smelt noticeably manly or slightly 'goaty'. And CNR showed it was in touch with the people by offering the essences for personal trial. Smell like Caesar! It was quite a temptation. And it proved to be quite a surprise, too, when the whole bus turned to stare and you needed four days to get rid of the scent of Eau de Générale.

Ellen Gross confined her researches to Poppaea, and the results are slightly more pleasant. Of course there's an asses' milk bath among her stock, but you don't need to rush out and milk 500 asses for it—100gms of essence will do for 100 litres (26½ gallons) of water. Rose oil, face masks, avocado cream, and hand balsam are on offer—in other words, just the kind of things Mrs Emperor or Madame Nero had in their bathroom cupboards.

Turn to the left and go up the Via Cavour, passing from Trajan into Christianity. The saintly Gregory the Great (590–604) marvelled at the forum, then still intact, and at the 'gentleness and righteousness' of its builder. A heathen, for whom heaven would always remain closed—he was greatly moved by the thought; he went into the Church of Saint Peter and wept bitterly for the Emperor's mistaken belief. And lo, a voice spake from heaven: 'Your prayer is answered; I have spared Trajan from eternal suffering. But make sure you don't pray for any more condemned souls in future!' In other words, not only was the Roman emperor God, but God must also have been a Roman, from the way he answered the tiresome pope—still a typical turn of phrase today: *però non rompere più*—just don't do it again!

In the same street, Via Cavour 313 is one of the best wine dealers in Rome and also serves excellent snacks (12.30–2.30pm, 7.30pm–1.30am; closed Sunday and in August). Michelangelo's Tomb of Julius II, in **S Pietro in Vincoli**, can be reached by crossing the Via degli Annibali, and ascending the steps on the right (signposted) through an archway. This is a work whose background has more than meets the eye in its appearance; it took 40 whole years, starting in 1505, to finish. *La tragedia della sepoltura*, the tragedy of the tomb, was Michelangelo's name for the drama depicted here, and the monument originally planned for the apse of St Peter's, freestanding with around 40 figures, shrank and shrank, although the master himself sought out the marble in Carrera. The result of S Pietro in Vincoli (St Peter in Chains—the reliquaries from Jerusalem and Old Rome are displayed on the high altar) turned out rather more modest than planned, as Michelangelo only worked on three figures personally—Lea praying (left), the charming Rahel (right), and Moses in the middle, dominating the group with his fierce gaze and stone tablets.

What happened to him? He was on Mount Sinai, where God ap-

Mercantile Rome

Michelangelo's *Moses*

peared to him in the form of a burning thorn-bush. At least, that's what the Bible says. And so Peterich pronounced him a 'man who has seen God face to face, the God whose image we may not make . . . is it not as if his eyes were fixed on this far distant picture?'

Israel's law-giver, according to Rolf Schott's *Michelangelo*, makes one realise that the creator of this sculpture was driven by the urge to strike the inner core of an entire mountain out of the rock by hammering and chiseling—to extract the spirit of the mountain'. You feel like asking 'is he going to start yodelling?' And to add one more disrespectful remark to the range of interpretations, the expression of the body-building prophet reminds me more than a little of Arnold Schwarzenegger; he always looks as if someone's stolen his sweets.

Left from the church door is Via Eudossiana. Empress Eudoxia presented the chains which had bound Peter in Herod's prison to Pope Sixtus (432–440), and paid for the church to be built. We'll stay on top of the Colle Oppio, with the Colosseum on our right, for a view of the remains of Trajan's baths. A walk through the park leads over the top of Emperor Nero's subterranean **Domus**

A break from sightseeing

Aurea, then down the steps to the Via Labicana and the **Church of S Clemente**.

Yet again, layer upon layer of deposits and remains, and if you want to map the passing of time, you should start with the lower church (4th century): a well-preserved Mithraeum, complete with the rushing sound of the Cloaca Maxima as sound effect, plus Romanesque frescos depicting the transport of St Clement's corpse and the miracles he worked. On the bottom of the Black Sea—according to one of the frescos in the vestibule—is the chapel where Clement was buried.

The church was rediscovered in 1857; it had been covered in rubble and completely forgotten when the new church was built in

the 11th century. The mosaic in the apse sets the Redemption in a Garden of Eden. The Cross is growing out of a healthy branch of acanthus; twelve white doves perch upon it. Christ stands before it, with Mary and Joseph at one side, like miniatures. Deer at the spring, peacocks, Doctors of the Church and all the events of the Gospels are framed in ornamental foliage. The choir in the centre is mostly from the lower church (6th century) and is one of the finest works of mediaeval art in Italy. The Cappella di S Caterina (to the right of the entrance) was painted in 1431 by Masolini and includes scenes from St Catherine's and St Ambrose's lives. This masterpiece of the early Renaissance has been restored and now glows with a tender radiance.

For those who want to eat in the area: **Ai Tre Scalini—Rossana e Matteo** has excellent ravioli with artichoke sauce, breasts of snipe with black truffle and similar delicacies, even if the price is a touch on the exorbitant side at 80,000 lire (Via dei SS Quattro 30, closed Saturday lunchtime and Sunday).

Day TRiPS

11. The Etruscan Trail

The parlour of the Etruscan family of Matuna of Cerveteri. Erotic games in the tombs of Tarquinia. A miraculous bridge in Vulci—30.5m (100ft) high, 2,300 years old. Etruscans just like you and me. Full day.

Railway stations: Cerveteri and Tarquinia, Rome—Pisa line; overland bus: Acotral Company, dep. 'Lepanto' (Underground A); Vulci for anyone with a car who likes walking.

'May we come in, Mrs Matuna?' There isn't a bell at the door, but the name-plate is there. To the left of the mighty oak in the necropolis of Cerveteri is a flight of steps leading downwards. The glass door is closed (visitors' breath was damaging the plasterwork), but there's a light in the parlour. Here you can see what a well-to-do Etruscan household looked like.

They were easy-going, these Matunas, that much is sure. No fridge, no washing-machine, but otherwise they took everything that makes life pleasant along on their journey across the big river—in the form of painted plaster that looks even more lifelike than the real thing. In the darkness under the earth seeming is more important than being. At the pillar there's a realistic assortment of tools—the sharp butcher's knife makes you notice the long neck of the goose playing with the greyhound on the floor.

The housewife's pots and pans, the husband's armour. The interior of their palazzo has architraves and a panelled ceiling and the alcove has two cushions. A family with some status has money, which is kept in the strong-box; on top lies the household accounts book—some

An Etruscan Tomb in Cerveteri

book-keeping is necessary, after all. The grave is a 'stronghold of life and death'; the daemon Scylla and three-headed Cerberus guard against evil spirits. The old Caere—eight temples, three harbours, 71km (44 miles) of coastline—traded with Greeks and Carthaginians. The fine grave objects from foreign parts still cause a breath of the big wide world to waft through the mighty tumuli, cylinder-shaped grave-mounds up to 30.5m (100ft) in diameter.

Written records have not survived, but the necropolis remains as the Etruscans' history-book; everyone was buried in the same style as he or she had lived. When the princes' might gave way to an oligarchy of rich merchants, grave design abandoned the tumuli in favour of straight, almost baroque façades carved out of tufa; the principle of equality is expressed in the distance between the doors in the 'terraces' and in their forms. Mr Average, on the other hand, was buried in stacks up to six layers deep. **Tomba dei Rilievi** (the tomb of Matuna with relief work), **dei Capitelli, dei Letti Funebri** (death-beds), **del Triclinio** (dining-room) and so on—no two tombs are alike, and the masons created mini-apartments with columns, flutings, ornaments and furniture, which to our eyes today are models of environmental art.

That sweet yearning for graves—if you want to continue listening to the throbbing harps of the soul, go left at the exit and along the fence; continue along the road that led from the piazza in Cerveteri. There are an estimated 40,000 graves here, many of which are still undiscovered. If you see fresh traces of digging further on, the *tombaroli*, the illegal diggers, have been at work, those arch-enemies of archaeology; nowadays a science concerned more with piecing together the lives and surroundings of the dead from their grave-offerings than with collecting attractive finds. The *tombaroli* destroy the unity of the remains. But still, there are mu-

seums (eg Paul Getty's in Malibu and in Basle) which the Italian police say are supplied by the black market and which are unable to produce proof of the origins of their exhibits. On the right, the road leads down to the underworld (**Via degli Inferni**), a tunnel ringed by graves. Back in Cerveteri, the **Museum in the Castello** (open winter 9am–4pm, summer 9am–2pm) has an exhibition of the objects Etruscans placed in the graves of their loved ones from the 9th to the 1st century BC. The trattorie **Al Cacciatore** and **Roma** are well-mannered country-style: fettucine, lamb, pork. 25,000 lire. If you have a car and like the idea of fish: **Nazareno** (località San Paolo, 50,000 lire)

Every Etruscan city has its speciality; with Cerveteri it's architecture, Vejo has ancient gods, in Tarquinia there are tombs painted in fresco. The mediaeval town of **Tarquinia** can be reached by motorway and the Via Aurelia. **Palazzo Vitelleschi** at the entrance has a museum (open 9am–2pm); stupendous gold jewellery, sarcophagi, a terracotta relief with two winged horses, a visible link with the character of Renaissance art. Ask at the ticket office for a guide to unlock the upper floor with the reconstructions of the tombs. Here are scenes from Etruscan everyday life—feasting, hunting, fishing, sports. And this time you can examine a house with architraves and painted ceiling—and inhabitants. Yet another declaration of love for life on earth, unrolling in the conflict between gods and devils, angels and demons (the other subject of the frescoes). You can also go on a tour of the tombs; in the **Tomba dei Tori** (bulls) there are figures of a man with another man, two men with a woman, in short, 'obscene groups' which have offended many a blinkered classicist. The Etruscans, porn fans? Tempora mutantur...

Both the Etruscans and the Romans had great respect for fertility, and thus they did not count the representation of copulation or genitalia as an indecency. Quite the opposite, in fact; they were a weapon against evil spirits, which could be rendered powerless by being insulted or being made to laugh. Everything which encouraged basic urges was efficacious against the evil eye and witchcraft, which explains the stone phalli on men's graves in Cerveteri (women's tombs have a small stone house), and the paintings of Tarquinia. When you see an Italian make the sign of the *corna* (horns) with his little finger and index finger—a double phallus—or the delta of Venus *(fica)* with thumb and index fingers—you know that the Etruscans are still alive and well!

Tarquinia has some interesting mediaeval churches, **S Maria di Castello**, **S Pancrazio**, **S Francesco**. Good provincial restaurants in the town, too and even better ones on the sea: **Girardengo** (Strada Litoranea, 12km/7½ miles, closed Tuesday and in November), **Gradinore** (Tarquinia Lido, closed November–Easter), **Velca Mare** (Tarquinia Lido, closed Tuesday, in November and December)—all around 50,000 lire.

Take Via Aurelia towards Grosseto and pass Montalto di Castro until you get to the turn-off to the right signposted to 'Vulci'. Another 9.5km (six miles) or so and you're at the Etruscan-Roman **Ponte d'Abbadia**. Inside the solid fortress of black stone (11th century) is the museum (open 9am–1pm, 2.30–4pm) with more recent finds. To walk to Old Vulci, keep left after the bridge (30.5m/100ft high, still testifying to the skill of its builders today) and go along the edge of the fields. The stalactites you can see on the other bank of the River Marta are limestone deposits from the ancient water systems. The only problem is a steepish climb down a slope covered in graves and a stream to be crossed. Cross an enormous meadow to the ruins (temple, cryptoporticus, mosaic floors, cobbled Roman street) of Vulci, conquered by the Romans in 290BC. If the watermark is low and you want to ford the river, you'll find around 20,000 graves on the other side, the finds from which are scattered all around the world (including the Museo Villa Giulia and the Vatican). The **Cuccumella** is the biggest Etruscan hill grave and is 150m (492ft) in diameter. It was once overshadowed by a high tower, whose foundations can still be seen.

Whatever side you're on, back to the fortress and the car. You need stout shoes for Vulci. Of course, it's also possible to spend a whole day just exploring this isolated area with its beautiful scenery, and take a second day to visit first Tarquinia (because of the museum opening times) and then Cerveteri. It's also worth going to **Tuscania** from Tarquinia, with its two magnificent Romanesque cathedrals—S Pietro, dating from the early 13th century, was built on the ruins of the Etruscan acropolis—and the **Tomba della Regina** (queen). The sarcophagi of the Kurunas family are in the **Bishop's Palace**.

If you have a car and you want to go bathing along some of Italy's loveliest beaches, head through Orbetello and Talamon out to **Alberese**. Go left along the lonely kilometres of shore, all protected as a nature reserve. Rocks, sand-dunes, pine trees— just as it was in the time of Odysseus.

12. In Italy's Wild West

The smiling Lake of Bracchiano is an enticing spot for bathing. Romantic ruins in Monterano, a little town on the southern edge of Maremma, abandoned in 1797. The Wild West of Italy—with real cowboys. Full day.

Bracchiano is the name of the railway station on the Rome–Viterbo line. Canalae Monterano can be reached by Acotral bus, departure more or less every hour from Via Lepanto (underground A 'Lepanto'). Both places can be visited in one day by car, but if you're using public transport you will have to choose between Bracchiano (swimming) and Monterano (walking).

Ruins—how romantic! Lords and princes once used to have artificial ruins placed in their gardens; it's a well-known fact that awareness of the past increases one's sense of well-being in the present. So all that crumbling masonry isn't just aesthetic nostalgia; as the writer Dino Buzzati says, it also contains a scrap of the spirit of the past, whispering its soft music, and you can hear its sweet song—if you pin your ears back.

Try it in **Monterano**. Is it the spirit you can hear rustling through the ruins in the forest—or is it the wind? Whichever it is, this elegy in stone is completely authentic—and pretty damn lonely. The bones of the **Palazzo Baronale** are the first you see lurking in the foliage—but I should tell you how to get there first, I suppose. Drivers go past Bracchiano (not through the town) to Manziano, left at the traffic light towards Tolfa-Civitavecchia, and right after about 4km (2½ miles) to Canale Monterano; left around the church (signposted 'rovine'). From now on you're also joined by walkers. The old road leads to a crossroads, where there is a sign on the fence to the left, 'Al fiume Mignone'. *Do not* continue straight on—if you want a bit of climbing, follow the sign, take the next right downhill until you come to the car park. Go on until you notice bubblings and evil smells—sulphur springs and sulphur vapours. After the bridge, take the path on the right, which goes uphill to the abandoned town. The holes in the rock face on the other side are Etruscan graves, with an abandoned sulphur mine in the middle of them, as are the stables under the aqueduct, still in use today are also Etruscan in origin.

If climbing's not your line, go in the

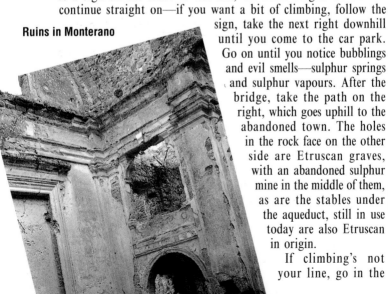

Ruins in Monterano

View from Monterano

opposite direction at the sign and cross country (actually heading past the ruins) to a metal gate. Go through the gate (closing it after you). After 183m (200yds) of car park the nature reserve begins. Walk further in the same direction to the viaduct. If you happen to meet an enormous bull with horns to match, don't panic. The Maremma bull, the Superman of its species, is harmless, just hope the bull knows this too. The herds are guarded by cowboys (*butteri*) on horseback, who are even lasso experts just like their transatlantic colleagues. A path leads over the rocks directly into the town; if you like, you can keep left first and then go right through what used to be the South Gate. The **palazzo** was awarded by Pope Clement X to his family the Altieri in 1671. Bernini carved the Lion Fountain at the front, of which sketches still exist. The lion was portrayed in the act of striking the rock with his great paw; from the fissure water flowed in an artificial waterfall into a basin.

On the right of the palazzo are the walls of the little **Church of S Rocco**, on the left the remains of the cathedral with a fragment of tower. Monterano was a diocesan town for 200 years. Outside the town walls, in a spectacular location on open ground, is the **monastery of S Bonaventura**, also designed by Bernini in 1763. The still-white baroque walls bear traces of 'black masses', fig trees and dung from the wild cows which shelter here in bad weather.

In 1799 the city was destroyed by the plundering troops of the French Revolution. The final impetus to move away for the 500 inhabitants was, however, the malaria which had ravaged the population for centuries; even the monks of S Bonaventura preferred spending the warmer months in Canale. If you haven't had enough of walking yet, go through the 'old Mill Gate' (back from S Bonaventura for about 46m (50yds), then left through the archway) and take the donkey-track into the **Mignone Valley** for more sulphuric eruptions.

Silhouetted ruins in Monterano

Retrace your steps back to Canale. You can eat elegantly in **Canaletto** (30,000 lire) or rustically in **Trattoria L'Alce** (25,000 lire). The Health Spa Association, 'Pro loco', has interesting information available, unfortunately only in Italian.

You can tell just by looking at **Bracchiano** that it was part of the powerful Roman church state for many years; a majestic castle overshadowing the mean houses and narrow streets, usually blocked with traffic thanks to post-war motorisation. However, the bank of the crater lake, 76m (250ft) deep, which supplies Rome with drinking water, has so far been kept clear of property speculators. In summer a little steamer sails across the lake between Bracchiano, Trevignano and Anguillara.

Castello Orsini is a real Aladdin's cave of art, a lovely view and an element of terror; a trapdoor to swallow up enemies, who were then minced by rotating knives; a little safe used to transport the lord and master's food from the kitchens—one's enemies never slept (tours Tuesday, Wednesday, Friday hourly from 10am–noon, and 3–5pm; summer also 6pm; Thursday and Saturday every half-hour, Sunday every 20mins, closed Monday and in winter).

Down on the lake, in the Vigna di Valle, is the **Museo Storico dell' Aeronautica Militare** (open 9am–4pm, closed Monday) of the Italian Air Force. Everything from hot-air balloons upwards—more fun than warlike. But swimming was on our agenda—from Bracchiano there's a path to the shore going down to the left of the castle. **Rari nantes** is the name of the official facility, but walk up the promenade to the left, and you can find your own private spot too. By car, take the road along the bank towards Trevignano, turn right before Vicarello, and you'll come to open shores with grass, willows and poplars. Noteworthy at Lungolago are **Il Luccio d'oro**, a family restaurant with sea-fish; the Bracchiano whitefish is known as *corricone*. And in the locality itself, fairly sophisticated: **La Trattoria del Castello**.

13. Mysterious Villas

A rose is a rose is a rose, but a villa isn't a house with a garden and swimming-pool. What is it, then? We reveal all in a visit to the Villa Adriana and Villa d'Este in Tivoli. Full day.

Acotral Bus: Via Gaeta (near Termini); private buses as well in summer, ask at CIT, Piazza della Repubblica 68, Tel: 67641.

Villa Adriana: Get a brochure with map at the entrance (open 9.30am–4pm in winter, 9.30am–5.30pm in summer; closed Monday). Don't take the metalled road, but foloow the path on the left that leads to and through the avenue, to the Greek theatre and the Nymphaeum with its plaster Venus (the original is in a glass case in the niche next to its copy).

Take a seat on one of the ashlars, look down into the valley and tell me what the river down there is called. Acquaferrata—or that's what it says on the map. Don't you believe it. You're in Greece, in Thessaly, to be precise, and you're surveying the Vale of Tempe so often eulogised in poetry. And you're not looking any more, you're contemplating. That was the way Emperor Hadrian wanted it, who had a high opinion of philosophy, and built his retreat here between 125 and 134.

When you look around, you could swear that he'd travelled the whole empire; **Tivoli** is a catalogue of fantastic travel experiences. After the avenue of cypresses, we find the **Stoa Poikile** (il Pecile) behind the high wall, the famous portico of Athens with its frescoes. The path leads past the **Small** and **Great Baths** to **Kanopos**, a canal in Alexandria. The **Torre di Roccabrunna**, a copy of the fountain of Timon which stood near the Academy in Athens, is an ideal vantage-point. Hadrian transferred the cradle of Platonic idealism to the top of the hill, in symbolic form rather than an exact copy.

Is the Villa Adriana the Disneyland of the ancient world? 'By

Jupiter!' Hadrian would curse into his beard—the first Greek philosopher's beard to be worn by a Roman emperor. This elite estate wasn't intended for the masses at all; in fact, the praetorian guard and the high wall made sure curious plebs never got near the place. And it's just this quality of being enclosed and cut off which makes a villa what it is—an oasis for the initiated, a Garden of Eden where it is always spring (there was always some flower or other in bloom), a refuge where man and nature, gods and the earth celebrated a mystical union—and an army of builders and gardeners were employed to make sure that all these wishes were converted into reality.

Hadrian's ideal empire contains some eminently practical buildings—for example the baths—and since it's well known that a healthy mind prefers a healthy body, a system of paths was laid out for joggers, riders and coaches which had nothing in common with the indecently bumpy surface of the consular roads. Temples, Greek and Latin libraries, various theatres, lobbies—the emperor's winter and summer palace offered all the comforts of the city without any of the noise.

The gardeners were no less masters of their art than the builders; the **Piazza d'Oro**, with its symbiosis of architecture, flowers and art (many statues now in the museum were excavated here), later served as an object lesson for the baroque masters. Borromini came here to study the dynamic lines which had replaced the severity of Augustan classicism.

But the villa and its park can tell us more still. They represent the character of an entire epoch, the picture-puzzle of its creator. Hadrian was a man of inner conflicts, drawn to the darker side of life. He ordered an artificial valley to be constructed, nearly 152.5m (500ft) long, between the Academy and the Piazza d'Oro, dubbed it 'the Underworld', and placed a statue of Cerberus, the three-headed dog, at its gloomy entrance to growl at passing mortals. The subterranean tunnel was 869m (2,850ft) long, dimly lit by daylight through 79 openings—a 'ghost train' for pedestrians.

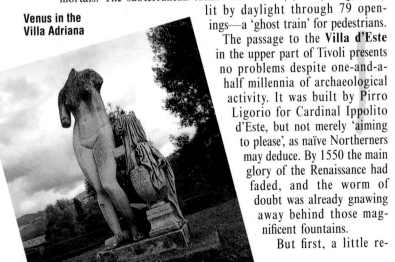

Venus in the Villa Adriana

The passage to the **Villa d'Este** in the upper part of Tivoli presents no problems despite one-and-a-half millennia of archaeological activity. It was built by Pirro Ligorio for Cardinal Ippolito d'Este, but not merely 'aiming to please', as naïve Northerners may deduce. By 1550 the main glory of the Renaissance had faded, and the worm of doubt was already gnawing away behind those magnificent fountains.

But first, a little re-

The remains of a temple in the Villa Adriana

freshment in **Adriano**, the restaurant at the entrance to the villa. When Marguerite Yourcenar was writing *The Memoirs of Hadrian*, she used to come here to coil Mamma Silvana's fettucine around her fork. The pasta *primi* (tortellini, ravioli, canneloni) are the 'hefty' dishes (60,000 lire).

Villa d'Este—you could say, decent paintings by decent painters (open 9.30am–4pm in winter; 9.30am–5.30pm, 8.30–11.30pm in summer). It's a lovely walk, but the real point is the garden, the pinnacle of natural drama—squared. It's a 'Yes, but' setting. Yes, because the 'religion of beauty' is celebrated once more, and is today possibly even more pronounced than it was in the 16th century; vegetation has covered the stones to frame the cascading fountains in lush green. Old engravings show a more rational, less wildly romantic *spettacolo*; although only a Monteverdi, Handel or Mozart of architecture could have devised so much *bellezza*.

The 'but' is there, because the beauty cannot be captured. The **Street of a Hundred Fountains**—magnificent. Ligorio's **Fontana dell'Ovato** (the oval) with its eight nymphs—high opera. 'But' step behind the flow, into a grotto like Hadrian's *Inferni*, and you enter into another world of darkness and death. The mannerist enters a cave to vanquish dragons and complete tasks required of him. He can do this and return purified to the light of day, but do we know that?

If you want to drive the Devil out, stick him on the wall. The dragon nightmare can be seen in the central fountain. Here's Orpheus, whose Eurydice died at the climax of their love and who sings to conquer the forces of darkness, the earthly hero of *bel canto*. Water is thirst-quenching, an essential element in washing, and glitters so prettily in rainbow colours when it sparkles in the sun. The Romans knew all this, which is why they built so many fountains. But even its liquid transparency can cast a shadow.

14. The Port

To Ostia Antica, the port of the metropolis of Rome. A look at everyday life in ancient times. Half a day.

Underground 'Magliana', change to the Ferrovia Ostia Lido to 'Ostia Antica', 10 minutes' walk to the excavated town. March–September also by ship, the Tiber II, from Porto di Ripa Grande (near Porta Portese), departure 8am, around 70,000 lire, including tour and lunch on board. Reservations: Tourvisa, Tel: 4463481.

Ostia Antica is a picture-book 'modern' town of the imperial era, even more so than Rome, which continued to develop while Ostia stood still (open 9am–6pm, winter 9am–5pm). A logical network of streets going off at right-angles from the **Decumanus**, the Romans' usual east–west main street. The Empire wasn't here to impress, but to produce and to trade to keep the overblown Urbs sated and quiet. Shipbuilders, merchants, salesmen, dock workers and customs officers were among the 50,000 inhabitants of this community which sank into the swamps and into malaria in the Middle Ages. At the beginning of the 19th century there were still about 100 convicts vegetating here.

The ruins encourage you to stroll around. No cars, just whispering pines, flowering oleanders and sermons in stones. The **Terme dei Cisari** (coachmen) immediately after the **Porta Romana** (entrance) on the right are testimony to the sweat of work and of travelling which the workers washed from their bodies as they entered the town. The (ancient) public lavatory (Via Forica) behind the forum, which makes all Rome guides turn their gaze (and their noses) away decorously although after 2,000 years it 'non olet' any more, is even cosier. The gentlemen of antiquity sat around on cool marble in a convivial semicircle. There is even supposed to have been a continuous flushing system. If that's not culture, what is?

Behind the theatre, capacity 2,700, although in those days it was bigger, is the business centre, with the trademarks of the 70 firms represented here in the mosaic floor. An institution which could also be found in Venice or in the cities of the Hanseatic League. A porticus for customers and passers–by and a public park enclosed the offices. The mosaics portray a chronicle of everyday life in Ostia—loading grain, ships sailing into the harbour.

Back to Decumanus, from which we'll keep turning off to the right; to help you decipher the inscriptions, *horrea* are warehouses, *fullonica* are laundries or dyers', *caupona*, *popina* and *thermopolium* restaurants and pubs, *tabera* are shops, *forica* are latrines. The museum has sarcophagi, busts of the emperors, and copies of Greek works. Down the **Via dei Dipinti** is a three to four-storey block of flats, with mosaic floors and frescoes testifying to respectable living. The **forum** was the administrative centre, the Capitol the financial. At Bivio di Castrum bear right to the Via della Foce, left to the Via di Serapide, left again for the Cardo degli Aurighi. On Decumanus go immediately right to the **Porta Marina**, behind which the sea used to come up. Back again, and now we'll tag on the other side of Ostia down **Via di Pomerio**. If you want to go swimming, take the Rapid Transit to the terminal ('Cristofero

Remains of columns in Ostia

Colombo'), or drive to one of the resorts. In Ostia Antica the fortification of Pope Julius II still stands, one of the earliest of all military constructions. It was built specifically for use in cannon fire but never saw battle because the enemy always came from the north and overland.

The Ostia Lido has good restaurants; good fish at **Lungomare Amerigo Vespucci** 156, in **La Capannina a Mare da Pasquale** (40,000 lire).

Nightlife

Turn night into day—it's easy in the mild Roman weather with its hot summer nights. *La dolce vita* begins at 10pm, and you may still find yourself stuck in a traffic jam on Lungotevere at three in the morning. *La dolce vita?* 'An invention, a myth', says Federico Fellini, 'I made the film, and then everyone started copying it.' So why not carry on looking through the spectacles he placed on all tourists' eyes? Like looking at Venice through the eyes of *Death in Venice*, or Dublin through the eyes of Joyce. Life imitates art.

What was it like in the late fifties? Sex kitten Anita Ekberg splashing around in the Fontana di Trevi for her softie lover Marcello Mastroianni. Ava Gardner having a fight with her friend Massimo Franciosa in the Via Veneto. Whacking and whisky—one bruises the skin, the other the soul. King Farouk of Egypt picking up the Capece Minutolo sisters in the Café de Paris and giving both of them a good time, although he—snigger—is hung like a flea. Playboy Dado Ruspoli, one of the 'black' (Church) aristocracy, casts stars and starlets aside as often as if they were used underwear. A time of adolescent passions; Peter O'Toole makes hospital fodder out of the photographer Rino Barillari (Fellini dubbed that whole breed of picture-hunters *paparazzi*). Frank Sinatra sends in his gorilla-like bodyguards to sort out the company of snapshoteers.

Sex kittens, stars and starlets, *paparazzi,* boys of both the play and whipping variety, and a few drops of blue blood to finish it off; everyone had a major part on the Dolce Vita stage—just like *Everyman.* The public, normal everyday people like you and me, sat outside the spotlights, shuddered in horror and gaped in fascination. Divas are as dead as dinosaurs, and for the same reason—no brain. Stars and starlets are thin on the ground—Rome's no longer Hollywood-on-the-Tiber. Playboys as the but-

terflies of the night don't turn anyone's head any more. The Via Veneto's a dead duck, full of tourists goggling at tourists, and Peter Secchia, the US consul, strolling around; who cares? Even Nadio Benedetti, director of the Hotel Excelsior and the Via Veneto Association, who would like to see the once glamorous street turned into a pedestrian-only area, admits that *la dolce vita* has turned sour. 'Fridays and Saturdays are when the 'troopers' come to town—guys with big jeeps and the stereo turned up high, who drive up and down the streets till three in the morning, blocking the traffic and bothering passers-by—especially girls.'

Curtain down? Not on your life. *La dolce vita* has moved, for one thing; and then, it's like money—you have it, but you don't flaunt it. Rome today is richer than it was in the fifties. Italians always did get rid of their repressions by going into the street and bumping up against people, but they're going for elbow contact nowadays like never before; you'll meet people wandering around at practically any time of night in the old city. You don't have to be one of the chosen few to live the *dolce vita* any more.

Hamburg has the Reeperbahn, Paris has the 'Crazy Horse' and other establishments where sex just ripples off the conveyor-belt, and Rome—has Rome. A couple of corners are like Soho used to be, namely Trastevere and the heart of the old city. But a relaxed dinner in the open air, a late visit to an ice-cream parlour or talking to your friends by a babbling fountain under the stars—all

Paolina Borghese

of this is *dolce vita* too. The night-life in Rome's is spontaneous and Dionysiac. The passage from a long night into the next new day, experienced in the company of others—that's one of its focal points. And the pleasant climate means you can be 'high' without needing to fill yourself up with alcohol. International trends don't make much impression on the Tiber. Punk, dread, house and other manifestations of the shadows are as rare as the proverbial talking dog.

The younger generation and naked sex: in the 7 o'clock performance in the dusty art deco picture palace of **Volturno** (Via Volturno 37, near Termini) you can watch this encounter. A porn film no one's watching, and a strip show where every seat is taken. A few Umberto Eco egghead types, a shy party of pensioners and a mighty gang of youths whose crew-cut hairdos betray a military precision—just the type that Fellini dubbed *vitelloni*, big calves. They're 'as canni-balistic as 500 sows' (Goethe). Not a repressed, isolated erotic experience, but an orgiastic declaration—as if the woman taking her clothes off was Santa Claus. Il Volturno is no Moulin Rouge, but pure tack, even if the amateur strippers are attractive—that just makes the whole tits 'n' bums *spettacolo* even more ludicrous. The main attraction is the audience. Some patterns of social behaviour seem to appear in every Italian, regardless of social status; when a pair of briefs hits the ground, there's a chorus of 'Bellissimooo', when a mount of Venus disappears from the spotlight, a cry of 'Bis' as if Pavarotti had just given of his best in a mighty aria. This childish joy in oh-so-sinful flesh is a delight, and every hand stays put—although they could touch if they wanted to.

Catharsis—purification—was the name the Ancient Greeks gave to the release of tension after the climax, and the army volunteers march off peacefully as lambs to the slaughter after the show is over. The men-only milieu of Volturno lurks on the fringes of society. Nevertheless, this group behaviour could be the key to the future, according to Michel Maffesoli, Professor of Sociology. 'After two centuries of rationalism, in which the Dionysiac principle was grossly neglected, suddenly orgiastic elements are making a reappearance in society.'

Take 'Woodstock', and the enthusiasm for live concerts which Rome shows as much as anywhere else.

But before we plunge into a sea of music, a short list of high-class establishments in the centre where film actors and actresses and society women such as Marta Marzotto or Marina Ripa di Meana hang out. **Divina** (Via Romagnosi IIa) is a disco and piano bar for an elegant collection of more mature guests who will also put on dinner-jackets and evening dresses for their special night out. 'Women on their own can also come here, and have a quiet evening without any of the stress of having to seduce someone the whole time. This I guarantee', announces the manageress Paola Lucidi.

GILDA
Via Mario de' Fiori 97
Disco and restaurant also aiming at the more mature, aristocrats and career women.

CASANOVA
Via Beccaria 229
Disco in Gabriele d'Annunzio style; curtains, veils, naked women on the walls, or as the manager Massimo Buonerba expresses it, 'a lot of sinful thoughts, and not much sin. Pity'.

OPEN GATE
Via S Nicola da Tolentino 4
Disco, cocktail bar

Piano bars with fashionable atmosphere in the centre:

LE CORNACCHIE
Piazza Rondanini 53
with restaurant

PIEDRA DEL SOL
Via L Santini 12, Piazza del Parlamento
Beer, crêpes, society jokes. Latin American music. Until 3am.

IL BATTELLO UBRIACO
Via Leutari 34; Corso Vittorio Emanuele
Beer, bar snacks and dancing.

The hot-spots of nightlife in the centre are: **Piazza di Spagna** (young foreigners from all over the world), around the **Pantheon** (the highest concentration of ice-cream parlours), and behind **Piazza Navona**, where the natives mostly go.

The Spanish Steps by night

Fonclea
Via Crescenzio 82a
One of the most famous jazz clubs in Rome. Generally foreign bands.

Hungry Bogart
Borgo Pio 202
Paninoteca—sandwiches in all variations—well known for lively music.

Quelle delle Notte
Via Leone IV 48
In 'Those of the Night' you can get delicious hot croissants, *cornetti caldi* (a speciality of Roman nightlife devoured after a good meal), ice-cream and also alcohol. Open until 7am.

Professionisti
Via Vittorio Colonna 32a
Hot croissants. Closed Monday.

Uonna Club
Via Cassia 871, further up the Tiber.
Hard rock. You might spot some punks here.

Piper 90
Via Tagliamento 9, on the other side of the city.
Great rock tradition. Disco, concerts, video hall, young people.

Saint Louis Music City
Via del Cardello 13, near the forum.
Jazz and (always a favourite in Rome) Latin American music.

A district all of its own for nightbirds is **Trastevere**, once the haunt of Bohemians and retaining its own special atmosphere. Few trendies, but students, artists and intellectuals.

Big Mama
Vicolo S Francesco a Ripa 18. Jazz.

Yes Brazil
Via S Francesco a Ripa 103
Samba, salsa and other Latin American music. Also for gays.

Blatumba
Piazza in Piscinula 20
Concert hall, drinks served during the performance. Latin American.

Definitely 'in' is **Monte Testaccio**, the first rubbish dump in history. In the 3rd century bc the Romans sited the city's provisions depot here and built enormous warehouses. Earthenware vases and amphorae which got broken eventually grew into a mound 46m (150ft) high and 1km (3,281ft) round, whose compactness is due to the ancients' hygienic habit of strewing everything with lime to keep down smells and putrefaction.

On one side is the former slaughterhouse, a piece of industrial history, and the former cattle market, now partially restored and today a stable for horses and coach-horses. On the other side are the music venues, burrowed into the mound like holes in cheese. From the Cestius Pyramid (underground B 'Piramide') and the romantic Protestant cemetery, where the graves of Goethe's son August and of Keats and Shelley can be seen) it's a fine walk in daytime, too; go through the gate into the courtyard and have a look around. In the evenings the 'Woodstock' people meet here to listen to the music. The pubs usually have several rooms, on the 'something for everyone' principle.

Carusso Caffe

Via di Monte Testaccio 36; a vaulted cellar with usually Latin American bands, a bar for chatting, a video room.

Caffe Latino

Via di Monte Testaccio 36: the mixture as before—jazz concerts.

L'Alibi

Via di Monte Testaccio 44: popular with gays and lesbians. Disco, salon, restaurant L'Eglise.

Radio Londra

Via di Monte Testaccio 56 : disco, bar, live music.

What does *il divertimento* cost? The tendency is towards free entry on weekdays; tickets (or, for clubs, membership) must be bought on Friday and Saturday. Competition is fierce, so places like **Casanova** or **Veleno** hand out free tickets in **Le Cornacchie** (Piazza Ronadini 53) or **Caffè della Pace** (Vicolo della Pace, behind Piazza Navona). In Trastevere and Monte Testaccio a drink—often a complicated cocktail—costs around 10,000 lire. When and where parties are on is divulged in the funkies' shop **Babilonia** (Via del Corso) and the **Jeanserie Bacillario**, Via Laurina 12, in **Eventi**, Via dei Serpenti 134, **Energie 1** and **2**, Via del Corso.

Caruso Caffè

Dining

'Tell me what you eat, and I'll tell you who you are'. To judge by that piece of wisdom (from Anthelme Brillat-Savarin), Romans are hearty, earthy people. A region's cuisine is the product of the environment and of history, and Rome's cuisine was determined by popes and aristocrats. They ate the more delicate parts of the animals, while the *popolino* had to make the best of the offal and coarser cuts. But necessity is the mother of invention, and Roman housewives and cooks have perfected their cuisine to such a point of artistry that the 'poor man's meat' has withstood all attacks by Italy's most recent economic upswing. The steak culture of big business and bigwigs hasn't been taken up by the 'man in the street'; instead, gourmets have devoted their skills to refining traditional dishes.

Start with the *primi*, the plate of Roman pasta. *Bucatini all' amatriciana* is a kind of fat spaghetti with a tiny hole through the middle, here served with a spicy tomato sauce and bacon. *Pecorino* (sheep's milk cheese) is grated over it. *Spaghetti alla carbonara*: bacon, egg yolk (still liquid), pepper and *pecorino* or Parmesan. *Penne all' arrabiata*: short noodles brought to white heat by *peperoncino*. *Spaghetti aglio ed olio*, with garlic and olive oil, and the possible addition of sliced peppers.

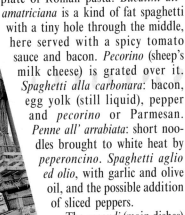

The *secondi* (main dishes) are also strong on emotion: *trippa* (tripe), *cervello* (brains, breadcrumbed and fried or in *padela*, with melted butter in the pan and peas, mushrooms or artichokes), *rognon-*

cino (sliced kidneys), *ossobuco* (knuckle of veal with mushrooms or peas), *amimelle* (sweetbreads). There are a lot of sheep around the Roman countryside, which leads to *agnello* (lamb), *abbacchio* (mutton) or *castrato* (castrated ram), grilled or as a highly spiced roast. *Saltimbocca alla romana* (veal escalope with a slice of ham, sage leaves and white wine sauce) is already on the way towards a more elegant and delicate cuisine.

Salads and vegetables are plentiful in and around Rome, since so much is actually grown there. Cheeses are also available in many variations. Mozzarella is the fresh buffalo-milk cheese shaped like a snowball—it should 'bounce' in the mouth. The same goes for

Fior di latte, a cows'-milk cheese, unfortunately available almost only in Rome and of very high quality. A new variety, and better than the French export of the same name, is the fantastic Camembert Italiano, which, alas, can only be found in a few gourmet delicatessens. Roman wine is fresh, young and white and comes from the regions of Frascati, Velletri or Marino and should be drunk early. Genuine trattorie serve it on draught. In more elegant restaurants, wine labels differentiate between *Vino da Tavola* (table wine, 80 percent of all wine produced in Italy) and *Denominazione di Origine Controllata* (possibly also *e garantita*), which are subject to stricter standards of origin and bottling.

'And I will greet you more heartily from today, ye inns/osterie, as the Romans so properly call you', lyricised Goethe, like the natives a classicist and not a Romantic. A typical Roman pub is furnished with tables and chairs and nothing else, and it has been threatened with extinction for the last ten years. The new prosperity, the siesta-less office hours through lunchtime and, above all, the new and unfamiliar stress have brought about a radical change in eating habits. It's not just the meteoric rise of hamburger joints

113

and the custom of many bars to serve *primo* and *secondo* as a quick snack for their busy guests. In the more bijou bars, the 'new cosiness' from Milan is spreading, with bouquets and dinky little candles on the bistro tables. It might be romantic, but it sure ain't Roman. The *nuova cucina* is fêted, and not without cause. It's founded on genuine research into the nature and origins of Italian cuisine. 'Quality is constantly improving, and there isn't such a big difference between Rome and Milan as the local patriots in Lombardy would have us believe', explained Federico D'Amato, head of *Guida dell'Expresso*, the best-informed restaurant guide in Italy.

Italian cuisine has great respect for its raw materials—it must be created without the need for nerve-racking alchemy, and be versatile enough for infinite variation and refinement. The 'Mediterranean diet' with its pasta, tomato, fresh herbs and salads and the finest olive oil, has a well-deserved reputation as well-balanced and healthy.

And yet there are fakes, gas-bags and thieves masquerading under the heading of 'Roman' too. 'In some cases Roman prices are justified, but most of the time they're exaggeratedly high, higher than in other European capitals. In Paris it's still possible to have a good meal for £13 or £14, ($26–28) but not in Rome', complains D'Amato.

Your 150,000 or so lire are well spent in REALIS LE JARDIN DELL' HOTEL LORD BYRON, which is probably the best gourmet restaurant in Rome under its chef Antonio Siullo (Via Giuseppe De Notaris 5, Tel: 3220404, closed Sunday). The menu varies according to the seasons, eg saddle of venison with chestnut purée or snipe in fig sauce, grilled figs, grilled boletus, croquettes of ground almonds and potato flour. And of course fish in endless variety, lamb and a magnificent array of home-made desserts.

EL TOULA (Via della Lupa 29b, Tel: 6873750, closed Saturday lunchtime and Sunday), the 'hayshed', is also an elegant place, and thanks to its many offshoots all over the world is like a 'mamma' for many an Italian manager. Venetian food, among other types, with a strong Emilian influence—the young chef Daniele Repetti comes from Piacenza. His *ravioli alla spigola* (sea-perch) *a sedano* (celery) with lobster butter, his juniper risotto and breast of pigeon, are all excellent. At lunchtime the menu *d'affari* is 60,000 lire, à la carte dinner up to 120,000 lire.

NEL REGNO DI RE FERDINANDO—TAVERNA DEI BORBONI (Via dei Banchi Nuovi 8) serves regional specialities, this time from Naples, in surroundings done out like a 19th century inn! 'O sole mio', or *linguine* pasta with a special *sugo di pomodoro*, mussels, fried fish and mozzarella (50,000 lire).

HOSTARIA COSTANZA (Piazza Paradiso 65, in the remains of the Pompeius Theatre, closed Sunday), has a menu ranging from Abruzzi to the sea. Marvellous meat, fresh fish from Porto Santo Stefano, truffles, boletus, home-made desserts. Without fish 60,000 lire.

And VECCHIA ROMA (Piazza Campitelli 8, closed Wednesday) is another 'atmospheric' restaurant surrounded by old palazzi, with tables outside in summer and a selection of 20 salads. *Spaghetti alla marinara* with scampi, *maltagliati* pasta with broccoli, *abbacchio*, squid. (60,000 lire).

PICCOLA ROMA (Via Uffici del Vicario 36, closed Sunday) in the shadow of the parliament, is one of the restaurants with solid, good food frequented by politicians. Roman cuisine, also fish (50,000 lire).

IL GIARDINO (Via Zucchelli 29, closed Monday) is a special tip with courtyard, not far from Via Veneto. A huge list of hors d'oeuvres guaranteeing a brilliant start and no waiting. *Tagliolini al limone, risotto al Barolo* (40,000 lire).

LA CARBONARA (Campo de' Fiori 23, closed Tuesday) is a regular haunt of the Romans because of its local cuisine. A speciality is *baccaià*, dried fish in a spicy sauce (35,000 lire).

What to Know?

Practical Information

GETTING AROUND

The Best Time To Go

When should you go to Rome? That all depends on you, for the Eternal City has something to offer in every season. The mimosa flowers as early as February; April, May and June are pleasant—although the spring is relatively short—as are September, October and November. If you're heatproof, go in July or August, when the city is half-empty, you don't need to fight for a parking space, and the baroque colours glow in the intense light.

Airport Connections

On arrival at Fiumicino airport, you can either take a taxi or—if saving money is important—take a 'rolling carpet' to the Rapid Transit station opposite (terminal Ostiense, Air Terminal; 'rolling carpets' also link up with the inland terminal). If your luggage is heavy it's best to call a taxi there. Buses into the city are not very convenient (716, 11, 92) and the underground station Piramide is a long way off—about 503m (550yds), although you're carried along for about half of that.

Money Matters

The semi-private banks usually offer the best rate of exchange, eg Banca Nazionale del Lavoro, Credito Italiano, Banco di Roma and Banca Commerciale Italiana. Monday—Friday 9am–1.30pm; 2.45–3.45pm. At Termini Station and Fiumicino there is a bureau de change open from 8.30am–7.30pm (closed Sunday). Larger hotels will change money in an emergency. All of the larger banks have cash dispensers, although not all accept foreign credit cards.

Clothes

Romans draw a clear distinction between the beach and the city; even on a boiling summer day, a native will not walk around in shorts and vest. And if you want to visit churches you mustn't be too lightly clad; St Peter's runs dress checks.

MINI-GUIDE TO THE CITY

The City of Rome is 150,219km² (580 square miles) in area and has just under 3 million inhabitants; a noisy, crude but also talkative and helpful little race (*popolino*). And the city's surroundings are as varied as the metropolis itself; if you're tired of town life you can be on the beach, at one of the three lakes or in the mountains, all in under an hour. There's usually a rather unpleasant breeze, and sensitive natures find the *scirocco* south wind particularly hard to handle; it covers the whole city with a yellow veil of Sahara sand. But the *tramontana* from the mountains sweeps the place clean again. It hardly ever rains for more than three days in a row—but when it rains, it really rains!

Rome is famed for its drinking-water fountains, bubbling with fresh spring water as clean as from the tap. And an excellent variety of bread is baked here, the *casa-reccio*, seldom found in other parts of the country. A less white version, the *integrale*, is also gaining popularity.

WORTH CHECKING OUT

What's On

You can find out the week's events every Thursday in the *Trovaroma* supplement with the daily paper *La Repubblica*. Over 100 pages of theatre and film premieres, opening and current exhibitions, concerts and operas, restaurant reviews from the beautiful people's hang-outs to fast food, nightlife, lectures and conferences.

Bel Canto in Caracalla

Roman opera is lethargic in comparison to Milan and La Scala. Once a year, from July to the beginning of August, the city wakes up and starts hitting the high notes in the Caracalla Baths. The greats from Verdi or Puccini with powerful casts; a real wallow in *bel canto*, plus—if Aida is on the programme and there's a circus in the neighbourhood—real live elephants.

Advance sales: Biglietteria Teatro dell' Opera, Piazza Benjamino Gigli. You'll usually be lucky at the evening box office in front of the baths, too.

The Beaubourg of Rome

Is it Rome's age, or its phlegmatic cultural policies? The community is governed by proportional representation, which usually doesn't bother about intellectual stimulation. With one exception—the **Palazzo delle Esposizioni** in Via Nazionale 194, a temple of the Muse from Victorian times, now restored and the scene of an attempt to emulate, albeit on a smaller scale, the example of Paris's Centre Pompidou. An oasis of calm on a listless or rainy day (there are such things), offering a collage of about three exhibitions, a caffeteria with a fine selection of salads and vegetables, a roof restaurant open until late in summer. Exhibitions open 10am–10pm, closed on Tuesday.

Getting The Creeps— Suffering Souls

Flirting with death, one of baroque's more macabre aspects. The Capuchins became specialists in joking with the *memento mori* (remember that you must die!) and designed crypts decorated with elaborate arrangements of corpses and skeletons. The collection of mummies in Palermo is fantastically sinister, but the Roman **Capuchin Crypt** (Via Veneto 27, 9am–noon, 3–6pm) is not much better. 4,000 deceased members of the Order, who died between 1528 and 1870, have had their bones fitted together like Lego bricks to form lamps, ornaments and altars.

Somewhat less ghastly is the revue of the poor souls, or rather their brand marks, which they left behind on earthly fabrics, books etc as a greeting from the fires of Purgatory. Pater Vittorio Jouet collected these traces and founded the **Christian Museum of the Hereafter** after the turn of the century; the museum is now in the Neo-Gothic church of **Sacro Cuore del Suffragio** on Lungotevere Prati 18. From Piazza Navona stright over the Tiber bridge, then right. It is open from 8–11am, ask in the sacristy.

The Flea Market of Porta Portese

One of the Sunday morning rituals is a visit to the Mercato di Porta Portese. It used to be known as 'flea market'; however, it's developed into a real second-hand fair, with everything from art and junk to cameras and stereo systems, plus all high-tech has to offer. Fabric and china, furniture and car tyres, you can always find something. Sustenance for this orgy of browsing is *porchetta* (sucking-pig), fritters and all kinds of Roman nosh. If you want to get rid of some money, best go before 8am; by 11 the first flush has gone. Parking spaces nearby are scarce—look on the other side of the river or take Tram 13, buses 23, 57, 92, 95, 716 (cross the bridge if necessary) or 26, 97, 170, 280, 718, 719 (from Trastevere). 10 minutes walk from the underground station Piramide.

The Botanical Gardens

The scent of the wide, wide world wafts through this oasis of peace in the middle of the city. Monetary inheritances may come and go, but this park, from the estate of the Florentine senator Tomaso Corsini, whose family provided the Papacy with Clement XII, grows on and on. Many arboreal patriarchs came to Europe in the footsteps of Columbus and Marco Polo. Exotic plants and blooms thrive in the glasshouses and are studied by the botanists at Rome's university. The refreshing walk through the Orto Botanico takes you up to the Gianicolo Hill with the **Fontana Paola,** as grand as the Trevi.

Villa Corsini, Largo Cristina di Svezia 24, open in summer (21 March–20 October) Monday–Saturday 9am–7pm, in winter (21 October–20 March) 9am–4pm. Glasshouses: Monday–Saturday 9am–1pm; 2,000 lire.

If you fancy a museum after all that fresh air, the nearby Via della Lungara, planned by Pope Julius II parallel to the Tiber so that pilgrims landing in the harbour of Ripagrande could walk to the Vatican as quickly as possible, houses in No 10 the **Gallery of Paintings of the Palazzo Corsini**, with Renaissance and baroque masterpieces (open 9am–2pm, Sunday 9am–1pm, 3,000 lire). On the way, in the Via della Lugara 230, is the Villa della **Farnesina**, with a collection of graphic art from the 15th to the 19th century (open 9am–1pm, entrance free).

ACCOMMODATION

5-Star Luxury

HASSLER—VILLA MEDICI
Piazza Trinità dei Monti 6
Tel: 8782651
The crowning glory: in the dining-room you hover above the Spanish Steps like a low-flying plane (single room: 360,000–380,000 lire, double: 520,000–560,000 lire, excluding breakfast).

HILTON
On Monte Mario, Via Cadlolo 101
Tel: 31511
Rome lies at your feet, and the prices of rooms with a view reflect it. Single: 370,000 lire (sans view from 275,000 lire), double: 520,000 lire (375,000 lire) excluding breakfast, but including park, tennis, sauna, pool and car park.

EDEN
Via Ludovisi 49
Tel: 4742401
The roof garden near the Via Veneto has a spectacular view over the Eternal City and luxurious conditions. (single: from 297,000, double: from 430,000, apartment from 750,000, suite from 950,000 lire—excluding breakfast, of course).

HOLIDAY INN CROWNE MINERVA
Piazza Minerva 69
Tel: 6841808
Extremely pleasant to stay in this newly renovated, elegantly furnished hotel; Stendhal stayed here. (single: 297,000, double: 406,000 lire, excluding breakfast).

Four-Star Hotels

FORUM
Via Tor de Conti 28–31
Tel: 6792446
Rome at its most Roman, between the

Colosseum and the Imperial Forum; fine view from the balcony (single: 270,000, double: 390,000 lire, excluding breakfast).

GIULIO CESARE
Via degli Scipioni 287
Tel: 3210751
If you prefer the Vatican district, you'll be well looked after hereas well as finding no problems parking (single: 260,000, double: 360,000 lire, including breakfast buffet).

RAPHAEL
Largo Febo 2
Tel: 6508852–4
Picturesque location behind Piazza Navona, front overgrown with ivy (single: 230,000, double: 360,000 lire, including breakfast)

CARDINAL
Via Giulia 62
Tel: 654 2719
In a fine old building with picturesque courtyard (single: 142,000, double: 238,000 lire, with breakfast).

SOLE
Piazza della Rotonda 63
Tel: 6780441
High-gloss hotel practically on top of
the Pantheon (single: 210,000, double
330,000 lire, including breakfast).

PLAZA
Via del Corso 126
Tel: 672101
Fin-de-siècle charm (single: 170,000,
double: 270,000 lire, inc breakfast).

DEI BORGOGNI
Via del Bufalo 126
Tel: 6780041
Recently opened, elegant hotel in the
heart of the city, marvellously peaceful
and excellent for longer stays. One-
room apartment with kitchenette/
bath: seven days 1.45 million, 14 days
2.45 million, four weeks 3.7 million
lire plus nine per cent VAT. Two-room
apartment (living-room and bedroom)
for same lengths of stay 1.9 million,
2.85 million and 4.65 million lire.

Three-Star Hotels

SCALINATA DI SPAGNA
Piazza Trinità dei Monti 17
Tel: 6793006
Attractively located above the Spanish
Steps (single: 131,500, double: 191,000
lire, including breakfast)

TEATRO DI POMPEO
Largo del Pallato 8
Tel: 6872566
A little jewel of a hotel in the winding

alleyways of Campo de' Fiori (double:
160,000, for one person 140,000 lire,
including breakfast).

RINASCIMENTO
Via del Pellegrino 122
Tel: 6874813
Run by Germans, central location (sin-
gle: 110,000, double: 152,000 lire,
inc German-influenced breakfast)

MANFREDI
Via Margutta 61
Tel: 3207712
In the artists' and antiques quarter
(single: 130,000, double: 200,000 lire,
including breakfast).

SAN CARLO
Via delle Carrozze 93
Tel: 6784548
In the pedestrian zone (single: 90,000,
double: 127,000 lire exc breakfast).

BOLIVAR
Via della Cordonata 6
Tel: 6791614
Near the ancient heart of the city,
own car park (single: 135,000, double:
193,000 lire, including breakfast)

LOCARNO
Via della Penna 22
Tel: 3610841–3
Art Nouveau building (single: 130,000,
double: 187,000 lire, inc breakfast).

CAPRICE
Via Liguria 39
Tel: 484812
Near Via Veneto (single: 68,000, dou-
ble: 108,000 lire, including breakfast).

Two-Star Hotels

CAMPO DE' FIORI
Via Biscione 6
Tel: 6540865
Small, but beautiful (single: 86,000,
double: 125,000 lire, inc breakfast).

CROCE DI MALTA
Via Borgognona 28
Tel: 6795482
In the shopping quarter (single: 90,000, double: 140,000 lire, excluding breakfast).

MARGUTTA
Via Laurina 34
Tel: 3223674
Simple, but central location (doubles only: 95,000 lire, including breakfast).

BROTSKY
Via del Corso 509
Tel: 3612339
Single: 55,000, double: 75,000 lire, excluding breakfast.

CESARI
Via di Pietra 89a
Tel: 6792386
Single: 100,000, double: 122,000 lire, excluding breakfast.

CASA KOLBE
Via San Tedoro 42
Tel: 6794975
In the shadow of the Palatine (single: 45,000, double: 66,000 lire, excluding breakfast).

Prices are correct as of January 1991 and rise annually by the amount of value added tax, in luxury hotels by 19 percent, in 4-star categories downwards by 9 percent.

GETTING AROUND

Traffic
Rome's traffic problem is hopeless, but not serious. As Dante announced at the entrance to the Inferno (to which Rome's traffic conditions belong), 'All hope abandon, ye who enter here!' And don't enter in the car, add the police, who have transformed the Capitoline, Palatine, Esquiline, Aventine, Quirinal and Viminal—in other

words, the Seven Hills—into a combination of fortress and labyrinth. It's hard to get in, and even harder to get out. So leave your horseless carriage in the hotel garage!

On Foot
The best way to explore the old city is on foot, especially since the pedestrian zones are constantly being extended.

Taxi
Taxis are rather more expensive than in some other European countries; they have to be yellow, otherwise you're dealing with a 'rogue taxi', seen mainly at the station and the airport; drivers usually approach you first. If you have to avail yourself of their services because there are no yellow taxis in sight or you hate the thought of waiting, make sure you arrange the price in advance; or if you can't speak Italian and the driver is asking you for incredible sums, put the hotel porter onto him. A legal taxi ride from Leonardo da Vinci Airport (Fiumicino) into the city should cost around 60,000 lire.
Taxi Call Numbers: 3570, 3875, 4994, 4517, 88177.

Bus
You can get to the centre with one or other of the many Roman buses, more like mobile sardine cans in the rush hours. Buy *biglietti* in the green kiosks at terminus stations and in some newspaper shops. 700 lire for travel on one route only, 800 lire for a ticket

which allows you to change and is valid for 90 minutes. Or a block of 10, for a reduction of 100 lire per journey.

Underground
Rome has two underground lines, which belong to a different company from the buses; bus *biglietti* are not valid in the underground. **Linea A** of the Metro(-politana) runs from near St Peter's (station: Ottaviano) to the Piazza del Popolo (station: Flaminio), Piazza di Spagna (station: Piazza di Spagna), Barberini, the main railway station (station: Termini), the Basilica of San Giovanni (San Giovanni) and Cinecitta. It intersects Linea B at Termini.

Linea B's route: Rebibbia, Tiburtina Station (Tiburtina), Piazza Bologna (Bologna), Termini, Colosseo, Circo Massimo, the Pyramid (Piramide), the Basilica di San Paolo (San Paolo), Magliana (change here for Ostia), EUR Marconi and Fermi.

A *biglietto* valid for both lines costs 700 lire from coin-operated machines or, in more important stations, in the kiosk at the barrier. A block of 10 costs 6,000 lire. The Rapid Transit from Magliana to Ostia Antica, Ostia Lido and Castelfusano (sandy beach) is also 700 lire.

Boat/Acquabus
A more peaceful—but not slower—way of travelling is the acquabus, departure every 20mins from the Tiber island via the **pier under the Ponte**

Cavour (same level as Piazza di Spagna) to Pante Amadeo d'Aosta (Olympic Stadium). The route passes through comfortable river scenery (and back, of course). 1,000 lire for half-way, 2,000 lire for the whole way. Cancelled at low tide.

Bicycle
A method of transport permitted in the pedestrian zones as well. Bikes can be hired out at Piazza del Popolo, Piazza di Spagna, Piazza S Silvestro, Piazza S Lorenzo in Lucina, Largo dei Lombardi and in the park of the Villa Borghese—4,000 lire for 1 hour or 14,000 lire for a whole day. Your passport will be required as a deposit. And check that the thing really works!

HEALTH & EMERGENCIES

Here is some information we hope you won't need to use: it's about hospitals. In the public Ospedali you are entitled to free **first aid**—eg in Fatebenefratelli on the Tiber Island, Piazza Fatebenefratelli 2, Tel: 5873299/5873324. The oldest hospital on the Isola Tiberina is said to have taken in plague victims as early as 293BC. In 1581 the monks of the Order of San Giovanni di Dio fitted it out so well with funds they had begged that every patient had a bed to himself instead of being shoved in with five others as was the custom. Sheets were changed so often in this hospital that the laundry bills were higher than the doctors' fees.

The private clinics (*case di cura*) are better turned out these days, but they want cash on the nail. **Salvator Mundi** has an atmosphere like a hotel and a beautiful site on the Gianicolo: Viale delle Mura Gianicolensi 67–77, Tel: 586041.

Emergency Telephone Numbers
Police: 113
Carabinieri: 112

Fire Brigade: 115
Traffic Police: 5544
Ambulances: Red Cross, Tel: 5100
**Emergency Service for Poisoning
Cases:** Tel: 490663/3054343
24-hour medical assistance:
Tel: 4826741
The Embassies will give you details of
English-speaking doctors and provide
assistance in the case of loss of pass-
port/money etc. At all strategic points
in the city centre there are police buses
with multilingual staff.

HOLIDAYS & OPENING TIMES

Official Holidays

1 January	New Year's Day
6 January	Epiphany
Easter	
25 April	Liberation Day
1 May	
Whit Sunday (Whit Monday is not a holiday)	
15 August	The Assumption of Mary
1 November	All Souls' Day
8 December	Feast of the Immac-ulate Conception
25–26 December	Christmas

Feast Days

Romans celebrate as and when they
feel like it, so the official calendar is
not madly interesting. In the Trionfale
quarter St Joseph is celebrated on **19
March** with fritters and doughnuts in
the streets. **At the end of June** (23/24)
St John is honoured by feasts of snails
and pork specialities (*porchetta*). And
between the two is the **Good Friday
procession** from the Palatine to the
Colosseum.

The traditional *urbi-et-orbi* blessing
is on **Easter Sunday** on the stroke of
twelve noon in St Peter's Square. The
banks of the Tiber around the Ponte
Cavour come alive in **June/July** with
a crafts fair of all the regions in Italy.
In **July/August** the summer festival,

Estate Romana, breaks out with public
concerts, dancing in the park, and
theatre/ballet/classical music in the
gardens of the various cultural insti-
tutes of Germany, France and Spain.

At Christmas there is always an exhibition of cribs from all over the
world, and from the beginning of December to Epiphany (6 January) is the
traditional but extremely commer-
cialised **Christmas Market** on Piazza
Navona. On New Year's Eve fireworks
are let off; fortunately, the old custom
of throwing china or heavy objects
out of the windows to express joy at
the turning of the year is gradually
dying out; strolling around became a
matter of life and death.

A permanent fixture for all-year fun
is the **Luna Park** in the suburb EUR
(on the underground line B), a funfair
with Big Wheel, ghost trains and
roller-coasters. 10,000 lire will just
roll out of your pockets. (Luneur, Via
delle Tre Fontane, Tel: 5925933, open
9am–8pm, on holidays and the evenings before them till 10pm, closed
Tuesday)

Opening Times

The elegant shops in the centre are open from 9 or 9.30am to 7 or 7.30pm and on Saturday in summer until 1pm, in winter until 7 or 7.30pm. They are not open Sunday and they do not open until 3.30pm on Monday. However, grocers and family bars still keep the traditional opening times: 8 or 9am–1 pm, 4–7.30pm. Rush-hour is between 8.30–9am, 6.30–8pm.

COMMUNICATIONS & MEDIA

Telephone

The much-feared *gettoni* (telephone tokens), which were always in short supply, are gradually dying out, and the old telephones with them. Caffè bars, pizzerias and telephone boxes favour the new bright red instruments which can be used either with the old telephone tokens, or with a 200 lire piece or two 100 lire coins. Some of them even take cards, available at newspaper stands or tobacconists' (look for the T, which stands for *tabacchio*) for 5,000 or 10,000 lire. Telephone centres, also for operator-connected international calls, are at Termini Station and in the main post office at Piazza S Silvestro, among other locations.

Stamps

Only sold in tobacconists' or post offices. The red post-boxes in almost every piazza have two slits—the left-hand one for letters to destinations within the city (*per la città*), the right-hand one for everywhere else (*per tutte le direzioni*). If you don't trust the Italian postal system (and you may be right), you can leave cards and letters at the Vatican post office to be franked (on the right behind the colonnade or at the mobile counter on St Peter's Square).

Foreign Newspapers

Newspaper stands at points frequented by tourists usually have foreign newspapers—eg Piazza Navona, Piazza di Spagna, opposite the Piazza Colonna, Via Veneto, the station and the airport.

USEFUL INFORMATION

Theft

Please excuse me for giving you a lecture on security. Don't hang bags on trolley hooks at Termini Station; concerted theft campaigns are frequent. Someone asks you something or pushes against you, the second whips the bag, the third runs away with it at top speed. These thieves are often North Africans. And another warning which may sound racist, although it's not meant that way: watch out for begging gipsy children! Especially when they come towards you holding out newspapers or cardboard boxes—don't let them get too close, they're the fastest and lightest-fingered pickpockets in the world!

Only take your passport along and as much money as you need for one day—leave the rest in the hotel safe! And full buses are often the haunts of professional pickpockets; hide everything so that not even the most skilful fingers can reach it. Don't wear excessive amounts of gold and jewellery, either. But you don't need to worry that the Romans are in a perpetual state of fear and trembling; they're so used to these precautions that they've become second nature.

Photography

It's completely forbidden to take flash photos in State museums except of sculptures, and in the Vatican museums not at all. You usually need the permission of the museum director to use a tripod. In the Sistine Chapel all photography is forbidden.

Tipping

Be generous with your *mancia*. Italy is expensive, and Roman wages aren't the highest. In ristorantes and taxis about 10 percent of the total is the normal tip. Of course, if your beer served at a table in a street café on Piazza Navona costs 10 times as much as the 1,200 lire it would cost at the bar, you can be rather meaner with your tips.

In hotels, you usually give at least 1,000 lire for carrying luggage and for the chambermaid (per night). Round it up for the porter, depending on how many extras he's got for you. And a well-worn truth—tips given on arrival have more effect than those given on departure.

If a verger opens up a chapel specially for you or a museum attendant draws your attention to a particularly attractive item on display, give him a nice surprise and press 5,000 lire into his hand.

The Pope

The Pope is one of Rome's living attractions. John Paul II's general audiences usually take place on Wednesday at 11am in the audience chamber (from November–February) or, from March–October, in the afternoon on St Peter's Square, sometimes in the basilica. Entrance tickets should be reserved in writing to be on the safe side.
The Prefettura della Casa Pontificia, reached by crossing the Portone di Bronzo on the right of St Peter's, issues tickets on Tuesday from 9am–1pm and Wednesday from 9am to

shortly before the start of the audience. On Sunday the Pope gives a blessing from the window of his study high above St Peter's Square (on the right-hand-side, looking onto the basilica).

Prices

Hotel and restaurant prices have risen ahead of the official inflation rates in the last few years. Watch out if you want to enjoy your cappuccino or aperitif sitting at a table: you'll usually have to pay double for service. Ask beforehand to avoid problems.

Tourist Information

From Ente Provinciale per il Turismo, Via Parigi 5, Stazioni Termini, or from CIT, Piazza della Repubblica 68—all have free information in English.

Consulates

Australia
Via Alessandra 215. Tel: 841241.
Canada
Via Zara 30. Tel: 8441841.
Ireland
Largo Nazareno 3. Tel: 6782541.
United Kingdom
Via XX Settembre 80a, Tel: 834194.
United States of America
Via Vittorio Veneto 121. Tel: 4674.

NOTES

ART/PHOTO CREDITS

Director	**Hans Höfer**
Design Concept	**V Barl**
Cover Design	**Klaus Geisler**
Cartography	**Berndtson & Berndtson**

PHOTOGRAPHY

	Elvira d'Ippoliti *and*
3, 6, 12, 14, 15, 16т, 17, 18, 19, 22, 26, 27, 28,	**Mark Aurel Rettenbacher**
35т, 36, 37, 38, 39, 41, 42, 43, 44, 45, 46, 56,	
57, 62, 65, 68, 73, 76, 79, 80, 102, 103	
46, 47, 48, 49	**NTN Corporation, Tokyo**

ENGLISH EDITION

Managing Editor	**Christopher Catling**
Production Editor	**Gareth Walters**

NOTES

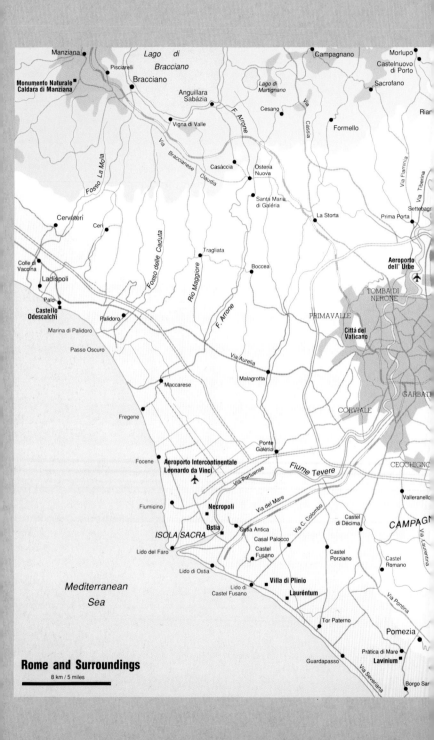

Manziana • Lago di Bracciano • Campagnano • Morlupo
Pisciarelli • Castelnuovo di Porto
Monumento Naturale Caldara di Manziana ■ Bracciano • Sacrofano •
Anguillara Sabázia • Lago di Martignano
Cesano • Via Cassia Formello • Riar
Vigna di Valle • F. Arrone Via Flaminia
Via Braccianese Casáccia • Osteria Nuova • Via Tiberina
Claudia • Santa Maria di Galéria
La Storta • Settebagr
Fosso La Mola Cervéteri • Prima Porta
Ceri •
Colle di Vaccina • Tragliata • **Aeroporto dell' Urbe** ✈
Ladíspoli • Boccea •
Palo • TOMBA DI NERONE
Castello Odescalchi Palidoro • PRIMAVALLE
Marina di Palidoro Rio Maggiore **Città del Vaticano** GARBAT
Passo Oscuro F. Arrone
Via Aurelia CORVIALE
Maccarese • Malagrotta •
Fregene • CECCHIGNC
Ponte Galétia • Fiume Tevere
Focene • **Aeroporto Intercontinentale Leonardo da Vinci** ✈ Valleranello
Via Portuense
Fiumicino • Via del Mare
Necropoli ■ Via C. Colombo Castel di Décima CAMPAGN
Ostia ■ Ostia Antica Via Laurentina
ISOLA SACRA Casal Palocco Castel Porziano Castel Romano
Lido del Faro • Castel Fusano
Lido di Ostia • Tor Paterno Via Pontina
Mediterranean Lido di Castel Fusano **Villa di Plinio** ■ Pomezia
Sea **Lauréntum** ■
Prática di Mare **Lavinium** ■
Guardapasso • Via Severiana
Borgo Sar

Rome and Surroundings

8 km / 5 miles